MW00609525

Chapin, SC 29036

Cover Design by Amy Rule
Design and Layout by Diane Florence
Project Editing by Susan Bowman

ISBN: 978-1-59850-121-6

Library of Congress Number
2012931289

10 9 8 7 6 5 4 3 2 1
Printed in the United States

Dedication

To the many students who helped to motivate and inspire me during my many years in Orange County Schools in Hillsborough, North Carolina.

Acknowledgements

A special thank you goes to Shawn Hessee. His amazing story adds so much to this book. I would like to thank Angelyn M. Hall for letting me use her poem, *Choosing Sides*. This is the second time I've used her poetry. Also, a special thank you goes to Balazs Szabo for letting me use one of his fascinating stories from his book, *Knock in the Night* which is one of the most powerful books I've read. Finally, thanks to my wife Carlye and son Aaron who helped with editing and computer glitches.

About the Author

Tom Carr lives in Hillsborough, North Carolina with his wife Carlye. They have two children, Sarah and Aaron. Tom holds a Master's Degree in Counseling and Guidance from Syracuse University. He has been an elementary school counselor for over thirty years. He also has his own private practice, Carr Counseling and Consultation, Inc. and is an education consultant and workshop presenter for Developmental Resources, Inc. in Chapin, South Carolina. Recently he has developed a motivational program called "Got Grit?" Tom has presented over 400 workshops across the country and Canada for educators and parents. He has several articles published in journals, such as *Journal of Abnormal Psychology* and *the School Counselor*. This is his fourteenth book. Besides writing and reading, Tom loves running. In the last thirty years he has run over 41,000 miles and completed fourteen marathons. For more information about Tom, his programs, and his books go to **www.gotgrit.org**.

Tom Carr
P.O. Box 344
Hillsborough, NC 27278
(919) 732-7183

Table of Contents

Table of Contents *(continued)*

PREFACE

In 1998 Youthlight, Inc. published my book *Monday Morning Messages: 52 Stories to Motivate and Inspire Young People*. Although the book was widely-used in hundreds of schools around the country, it was written more for parents. It was designed to give parents one story a week to read to their children throughout the year. Because I feel so strongly about the art of storytelling, the publisher and I agreed to do some revisions of the book. First of all we wanted it to be more applicable for use by counselors and teachers. Parents will still find this new book very relevant for their children. Next we eliminated some of the previous stories and added fifteen new ones. Finally we've added more follow-up activities to enhance the stories. And, as you can tell, we've changed the title.

My wish is that educators and parents revisit the power of storytelling. Let's use a bit less technology and get back to the days when children asked, "Please tell me a story." I'm convinced that the stories in this book will motivate and inspire young people.

— Tom Carr

Introduction

CHANGING LIVES: ONE STORY AT A TIME

Yes, I truly believe that good stories can change people's lives. I've been a school counselor for thirty years and most of my classroom guidance lessons revolve around storytelling. During the last twenty years, I've never used one piece of technology in my lessons: no videos, computers, filmstrips, overhead projectors, iPods, Smart Boards, etc. I tell stories. Then the students and I discuss them and we talk about lessons learned and/or the morals. I believe kids learn more from stories than they will from lectures. I want the students to be fully engaged: laughing, getting angry, looking puzzled, or even crying. I want them to feel a full range of emotions. Not every one of my stories ends with a, "And they lived happily ever after." Life is full of hurt, disappointment, unfairness, as well as love, happiness, humor, and the bad guy usually does get caught. I let the children know if the story is true or not. I've discovered that when I tell them that a story is true, they seem to pay better attention. Lately I've noticed that students tend to enjoy an occasional gross-out type of story. Don't avoid books or stories about *Captain Underpants, The Diary of a Wimpy Kid*, or *Walter the Farting Dog*. I believe that many of my stories have had a positive impact on the lives of the students I've taught over the years.

Many years ago Norman Vincent Peale founded the magazine *Guideposts*. He realized how powerful stories can affect people. *Guideposts* is one of the top selling magazines in the country. Obviously millions of readers find the true stories to be a blessing. The magazine's description notes, "GUIDEPOSTS is a monthly inspirational, interfaith, non-profit magazine written by people from all walks of life. Its articles help readers achieve their maximum personal and spiritual potential." Today the magazine is headed up by Edward Grinnan. Recently he wrote the book, *The Promise of Hope: How True Stories of Hope and Inspiration Saved My Life and How They Can Transform Yours*.

A SIX-PACK OF MINI-STORIES

Following are six short stories. After each one ask yourself these questions. Would I tell this story to my class? Do I feel comfortable telling the story? Can I develop a few follow-up discussion questions? What lessons will children learn from it? What grade levels would the story be appropriate for? How can I use the story to help enhance students' social skills and positive character traits?

FOOD FOR THOUGHT

When the late and famous New York City Mayor, Fiorello La Guardia was serving as a precinct judge, a man charged with stealing a loaf of bread was brought before him. The man pleaded guilty, saying yes he had stolen the bread because he was hungry. La Guardia announced that he had no alternative but to fine the man $10, which he paid out of his own pocket. He then fined the courtroom spectators 50 cents each for living in a city that would force a man to steal in order not to starve.

— A.C. Snow, Raleigh News & Observer, Dec. 12, 2010

A FATHER'S INTEGRITY WAS AT STAKE

Mr. Smith took his identical twin 11 year-old sons, Nick and Nate, to a charity hockey game in Minnesota. He placed both their names in a raffle for a chance to win $50,000 at half time. During the intermission Nick's name was drawn from the raffle bucket. If he could hit the target with a puck from ninety feet away, he'd win. It was an almost impossible task as the 3-inch puck had to slide into a slot that was only 3 and a half inches wide, from ninety feet away! When Nick's name was announced, he couldn't be found so Mr. Smith told Nate to tell the director that he was Nick. Nate grabbed the hockey stick, slapped the puck, and believe it or not, he made it! $50,000 would be coming his way. Later that night dad tossed and turned in bed. He knew it was Nate, not Nick (whose name was drawn) that made the shot. The next morning he called the folks at the hockey arena to tell them the truth.

— ESPN News, Aug. 15, 2011

HE'S NOT OUR RESPONSIBILITY

Years ago federal laws forbade the transportation of lepers across state lines. Persons known to have leprosy could not cross state lines without written permission from every locality being traversed. State officials rarely consented. There was a Chinese student named Mock Sen who had been preparing to return home from the United States after attending college when he was diagnosed with leprosy. Officials stuck him in a freight car and used a pole to push food in after him. Sealing the car, they sent it down the tracks toward the next state. Local agents in the neighboring state had the car decoupled and routed back to its point of origin; authorities there promptly sent the railroad car away again. Mock Sen was shuttled around the country in a sealed boxcar for almost two weeks. Finally, a doctor insisted on entering the car. Mock Sen had been dead for days.

— John Tayman, The Colony, 2006

THE MOST ADMIRED RULE-BREAKER in AMERICA

J.P. Hayes was a 'middle-of-the-road' golfer who was having a decent year on the links in 2008. He was trying his best to qualify for the 2009 Pro Golfers Association Tour where he would have an excellent chance to win a lot of money. He was participating in a qualifying tournament in Texas when he had mistakenly used a non-regulation ball for just two strokes. Since the ball was unapproved for competition, Hayes admitted his mistake and was disqualified. No one else saw it and no one would have ever known. He said, "I violated a rule and I had to take my medicine." Hayes' behavior is a perfect example of one definition of character that states, "Character is what you do when no one is watching."

— ABC News, Nov. 20, 2008

I'VE SPENT A LONG TIME LOOKING FOR YOU

One morning when I went to say Mass at a mission chapel in Shinyanga, Tanzania, I discovered an inert baby lying in front of the altar. The mother, explaining that the little girl was dead, asked if I could say a Mass for her. Just then, the bundle moved. "She's still alive," I declared. "But she's sick and I have no money for medicine. She'll be dead soon anyway," the mother replied. Giving the mother ten shillings, I sent her off to a hospital with the baby. Seven years later a woman, waving frantically, stopped me on the road. Breathlessly she explained, "My little girl lived, and here's your ten shillings. I've spent a long time looking for you."

— Father Joseph Brannigan, Once Upon a Time in Africa, 2004

DID HE CHEAT OR WAS HE JUST FOLLOWING THE RULES?*

I love to tell people a story my mother recounted on birthdays. It was my favorite family story; a great tale of our Scottish heritage. It seems that the MacNeil clan chieftain, the story went, was feuding with another clan leader over ownership of an island. Rather than risk widespread death and injury, the two agreed to settle the issue in a competition. The two chiefs agreed to race in identical boats from the mainland to the island, and the man who first put his hand upon the island would claim the isle for his clan. In the early morning fog, the two men set out in their open boats. The race was a dead heat until the very end, when the opposing clan chief inched ahead. At the end of the race, with MacNeil a few boat lengths behind, the island looked lost for the MacNeils. As the other chief stepped out of his boat in the shallow water near shore, the MacNeil chieftain removed his blade and severed his right hand. He picked up the bloody stub and hurled it onto shore, winning the island for the MacNeils.

— Neil White, In the Sanctuary of Outcasts, 2009

**Author's note: I've told hundreds of stories to children and this is one of their favorites. Obviously you must determine appropriate age levels of the students. I tend to add a lot more information and details to it. Great discussion usually follows. Some students think he cheated but others note that he didn't; he followed the rules!*

HOW TO USE THIS BOOK

1. Read each story yourself.
2. Determine the appropriate age/grade level for each story.
3. Know your students well. For instance you may not want to tell a story of a pet dying if one of your students recently lost a pet.
4. After you've read the story and determined appropriateness, practice telling the story. You can add more to the story, fluff it up a bit, or eliminate parts. Then tell the story to your students; try not to just read it. Let the kids see your eyes, body movements, and gestures. Show excitement. Study your crowd. How are they reacting?
5. Let the kids know up front if the story is true, based on a true story, or fiction. Remember, true stories are more powerful. You can check the "Notes" section in the back of the book to see which of my stories are true.
6. If you are looking for stories on certain topics such as integrity, teasing, risk-taking, etc., you'll see that information in the "Table of Contents."
7. If possible, end each story with a discussion. Also, at the end of each story there is a follow-up activity that can be completed individually or in a small group.
8. Revisit the stories often. For example, if you find that students aren't listening well, ask, "Does anyone remember what happened to the man who didn't listen in the story, An Alaskan Adventure?"
9. Don't be hesitant to retell the same story occasionally. When I visit classes I often have students request stories that they've heard several times before.
10. Happy storytelling!

— Tom Carr

An Alaskan Adventure

Listening is a very important skill. Many people are able to master this skill, while others never learn. Parents and teachers are constantly reminding children to listen and pay attention. I always remind my students, "Good things happen to good listeners and bad things happen to bad listeners." Chuck was not a good listener and something very bad happened to him. Let me tell his story.

Chuck was a 35-year-old amateur photographer who had always dreamed of going to Alaska to take pictures. After several years, he was able to save enough money to quit his regular job and head to Alaska for a few weeks. Chuck never really took the time to learn much about Alaska before his trip. He was unaware of the extreme weather conditions, and the great vastness of this state. He thought he was prepared for his trip. As we later find out, he was not prepared.

A few days before leaving, he had to get his hunting and fishing license, and take a safety/rescue course. At the session, he never listened or paid attention. He thought he knew everything he would need to know. He should have listened closely to rescue information, but he did not.

A bush plane dropped Chuck and his supplies off in the middle of one of the most remote areas of the state. He forgot to tell the pilot when to return to pick him up. For the next few weeks, he enjoyed the great outdoors and took many beautiful pictures. Soon his supplies began to run low. He was running out of food and the weather was turning cold.

Chuck still assumed that someone would eventually find him. Surely a hunter or maybe another bush plane would pass his way. He was getting ill and weak and winter was close at hand. He began to really worry now. "Will I ever be rescued, and will I ever see my family again?" He could not hold out much longer.

As he was nearing death one day, he heard a plane. He dragged himself into an opening. The plane flew low and the pilot waved to him. Chuck was so excited that he raised his right hand in the air and pumped it up and down a few times just as a football fan would do after his team scores a touchdown. "I'm going to be rescued!" He went back to his shelter and started packing. Soon he would be back at home with his family. He waited for the plane to return.

Several hours went by, then several days went by, and the plane did not return. Chuck knew the plane saw him. "The pilot actually waved to me." Something is wrong he thought. He huddled in the corner of his small shelter trying to keep from freezing. He was now completely out of food.

A couple of more days went by without any sight or sound of the plane. With the last bit of energy he had, he took out his wallet to look at his family pictures one last time. He also took out his hunting license. As he read the back of his license, he discovered the reason for the plane not returning to help. On the license were drawings of emergency hand signals for communicating with aircraft from the ground. He discovered too late that raising a single arm is the universally recognized signal for "all O.K.; assistance not necessary." The signal for "SOS, send immediate help" is two upraised arms. Chuck used the wrong hand signal. He should have listened and paid attention when getting his license.

A few days later he died. We know the story of Chuck, because he kept a diary which was discovered from his frozen shelter. If he had listened, he would have survived, but as a result — his actions were fatal.

ACTIVITY 1: Practice Good Listening Skills

Directions: Pair up with another person. Take turns telling a brief story. One person tells the story and the other one practices the listening skills. Also, you may want to keep a copy of these skills in your desk.

Ten Skills for Good Listening

1. Sit up straight.
2. Use good eye contact. Keep your eyes focused on the person talking to you.
3. "Erase" the brain. Whatever the teacher is talking about, then that is what needs to be on your brain. If the teacher is explaining math, then math is on the brain. When math is finished, erase the brain and put the next subject on the brain. If your teacher is discussing science and you have thoughts of tonight's ball game on your brain, then you're not listening well.
4. Keep hands in control.
5. Stay on the subject. Bad things usually happen to bad listeners.
6. Ask questions about the topic or subject. Don't interrupt the teacher or ask questions until she has finished giving instructions.
7. "Act" interested. Even if you think the lecture or lesson is boring, try to act like you are interested and you may actually begin to listen better and learn more.
8. Use proper facial expressions. This lets the other person know that you really are listening.
9. Nod your head once in a while. This tells the other person that you either agree or understand what they are talking about.
10. Repeat or rephrase. If you listen well then you should be able to "put into your own words" what was said.

The Persistent Pooch

Jeff took a lot of teasing from his hunting buddies, because he was the only one without a dog. He had often thought of getting a hound, but was not that crazy about all the responsibilities that go along with owning one. After several unsuccessful hunts, he decided to visit Jake Reynolds, the owner and breeder of some of the best hunting dogs in the state. After looking over a litter, he brought home a puppy named Bo.

Bo quickly made the back of Jeff's old, red, rusty, Ford pickup truck, his home. All day long he would eat, sleep, and play in the bed of the truck.

Finally, the day came for Bo's first hunt. Jeff put Bo in the back of the truck, and headed for the mountains. Jeff parked his old, truck at the end of a dirt road. He grabbed his rifle, and placed Bo on the ground. Bo picked up a scent, started howling, then took off running up the hill. Jeff followed along. Bo kept howling, running, and barking. Soon it became quiet. "Why did Bo stop barking?" Where is he?" Jeff returned to his truck, and there was Bo sleeping in the back! The next time they went hunting, Bo did the same thing.

Jeff was frustrated. He paid good money for this dog, and all it wanted to do was sleep in the bed of his old truck. He thought, "What a lazy dog I have."

The next time out, Jeff tried something different. As soon as Bo ran off after a rabbit, he moved the truck a mile down the road. This plan didn't work. Bo howled and ran around as usual for a few minutes, and then it became quiet. Even though Jeff moved the truck — Bo found it, jumped in, and fell asleep!

Jeff was determined to break Bo of the sleeping habit. The following day, he loaded Bo in the truck and drove to the mountains. As soon as Bo ran off howling, Jeff spray-

painted his truck green, hoping Bo wouldn't recognize it. This strategy didn't work either. Bo returned, jumped in the back, and started snoring.

On two different hunts, Jeff tried to blindfold the dog, and once, he even put a nose plug on Bo. These plans did not work either. No matter what Jeff did, Bo always returned to the truck for a nap.

For several days Jeff pondered his problem. He talked to himself, "Should I give up trying to train Bo, take him back to Jake Reynolds, or trade in the old Ford and get a new one?" Even though Bo was a persistent, lazy dog, Jeff was actually starting to like him.

Jeff finally decided to trade in his old truck for a new one. He drove the ten miles to town to Buck Nichols' Ford City. With tears in his eyes, he traded in his old truck for a new blue model. Bo hated the new truck and refused to go anywhere near it. Jeff thought, "Now maybe Bo will stay on the trail and hunt, and not return to the new truck and go to sleep."

Early on a Saturday morning, Jeff had to force Bo into the front of the new truck. Jeff parked the truck along a dirt road and pushed Bo out. The dog took off howling as usual. Jeff waited and waited. The barking stopped, and Bo did not return to the new truck. "Has he found a rabbit or treed a raccoon? Has my plan to get rid of the old truck worked? Will Bo finally become a good hunting dog?"

Several hours went by and Bo did not return. When dark came, Jeff went home. He was very worried about Bo. "Where is he?" Three days went by and still no signs of Bo. Jeff missed his buddy.

After work one day, Jeff traveled to town to buy groceries. As he approached Buck Nichols' Ford City, he thought about his old truck. He decided to stop and see it one more time. There it was at the back of the lot with a "For Sale" sign in the window. He walked around it, kicked the tires, and patted the roof. As he stood there, he heard a strange noise — a snoring sound. In the bed of the truck was Bo, curled up and sound asleep! Even though the truck was parked ten miles from town, Bo still found it!

Jeff admired his persistent pooch. He bought back his old truck and parked it next to the barn. Every day now you will find Bo in the back of the truck. He never became a great hunter, but he became a happy hound. His persistence paid off!

You will be surprised at all that you can accomplish if you are persistent.

ACTIVITY 2: Terrible Tongue Twisters

Directions: Listed below are ten tough tongue twisters. Get with a friend or a small group of classmates and see if you can master a few of these twisters. If you are **persistent** you'll be successful. Also, you'll enjoy a few chuckles!

---

1. **Toy boat, toy boat, toy boat.**
2. **I saw Susie sitting in a shoe shine shop where she sits she shines, and where she shines she sits.**
3. **How can a clam cram in a clean cream can?**
4. **The thirty-nine thieves thought that they thrilled the throne throughout Thursday.**
5. **If Stu chews shoes, should Stu choose the shoes he chews?**
6. **Santa's short suit shrunk.**
7. **Eleven benevolent elephants. Eleven benevolent elephants.**
8. **A big black bug bit a big black dog on his big black nose.**
9. **Six slimy snails sailed silently.**
10. **The sixth sick sheik's sixth sheep's sick.***

*According to the *Guinness Book of World Records*, this tongue twister is considered the most difficult one in the English language.

Wilma and Glenn – They Didn't Run Out of Excuses

Have you ever noticed that there are many people who are very good at coming up with excuses? Whenever they fail at something, make a mistake, or do not achieve their goal, they come up with excuses. Sometimes they use so many excuses, that they reach a point where they cannot think of any new ones.

I overheard the following conversation between a teacher and a student:

Teacher: "Sam, this is the fifth day in a row that you did not bring in your homework. Why?"
Student: "Well, I...ah...I...well...(he couldn't answer).
Teacher: "What's wrong? Are you running out of excuses?"

Let me tell you about a couple of remarkable athletes who became two of the greatest runners of all time. Both had some very unfortunate things happen to them when they were children. They could have had hundreds of excuses for not being successful. Instead of running out of excuses, they actually ran over and through them.

Wilma Rudolph

Wilma lived in a very poor family with 21 other brothers and sisters. She was a premature baby, and at the age of four, she was struck with pneumonia and scarlet fever, which left her with a paralyzed left leg. At age nine, she was able to remove the metal leg brace she had been dependent on, and began to finally walk without it. By the age of thirteen, she decided to become a runner even though she hadn't totally mastered the skill of walking correctly. She entered a race and came in last. During the next few years, she continued to come in last in every race. Eventually she won a race. This girl, who was told she would never walk again, went on to become the fastest woman runner in the world in 1960. She won three gold medals in the Olympics!

Glenn Cunningham

In his book, *The Miracle of Motivation*, George Shinn tells this amazing story:

Glenn and his older brother had a job at the local school. They had to get up early every morning and start a fire in an old stove in the classroom. One morning the brothers cleaned out the stove and loaded it with firewood. His brother took a can of kerosene and poured it on the wood. He lit the fire with a match.

A large explosion rocked the school building. Due to a delivery man's error, the five-gallon kerosene can had been filled with gasoline. The fire killed Glenn's brother and left Glenn's legs badly burned.

The doctor told the parents that amputation would be the safest course of action. But the parents said, "No!" They had just lost one son, and did not want to see Glenn lose his legs. They asked if he could wait yet another day. And again the next day, they asked for a postponement. Soon the delay became a week, then a month and longer. The parents used the time to instill in the boy the belief that he would walk again someday.

When the bandages were finally removed, it was found that Glenn's right leg was two inches shorter than his left. The toes on his left foot had almost burned off. He was determined to walk again — and he did. First he used crutches to walk, and then he started running.

He kept running, and those legs that came so close to being amputated carried Glenn Cunningham to a world record in the mile run. Later he was called, "The World's Fastest Human Being."

Successful people seldom use excuses!

ACTIVITY 3:
Famous People...No Excuses!

Directions: See if you can match up the famous persons on the following page with the "negative" events that happened to them when they were young. These people became successful in life in spite of "bad" things happening to them. They didn't use excuses!

---

a) This person was told by a newspaper editor, "It is easy to see from your cartoon sketches that you have no talent."

b) This person was told by one of his managers, "You can't sing. You ain't going nowhere. You ought to go back to driving a truck."

c) This author of Little Women was told by her first editor that she would never write anything popular.

d) This *I Love Lucy* star was told by her high school drama teacher, "Try any profession but acting."

e) This person was cut from his junior high basketball team.

f) This person's music teacher told him he was "hopeless" as a composer.

g) This famous scientist was four years old before he could speak and failed college entrance exams.

h) This blues singer lived in poverty, and worked in cotton fields.

i) This group was told by Decca Records, "We don't like your sound. Groups with guitars are on the way out."

j) This actor was once told, "You have no talent!"

k) This diving Olympic gold medalist was adopted, had asthma, and a learning disability.

l) This founder of Wendy's restaurant didn't get his high school diploma until 1993, at the age of 60.

m) This TV talk show host was born out of wedlock, sexually abused, and sent to a juvenile detention home.

n) This famous poet was sexually abused as a child, and worked as both a waitress and a cook.

o) This author had an alcoholic father, his mother died when he was 2 and he was abandoned by his family.

_____ **1. Louisa May Alcott**

_____ **2. The Beatles**

_____ **3. Walt Disney**

_____ **4. B.B. King**

_____ **5. Michael Jordan**

_____ **6. Elvis**

_____ **7. Burt Reynolds**

_____ **8. Dave Thomas**

_____ **9. Maya Angelou**

_____ **10. Albert Einstein**

_____ **11. Oprah Winfrey**

_____ **12. Greg Louganis**

_____ **13. Edgar Allen Poe**

_____ **14. Lucille Ball**

_____ **15. Beethoven**

The Slave and the Lion

The Roman Emperor Caligula, was one of the cruelest rulers ever to live. On a regular basis, he would invite thousands of Romans to the Colosseum to watch trained fighters, called gladiators, fight each other, or fight wild animals. Quite often these battles would end in the death of a gladiator or an animal. Caligula would also throw prisoners and slaves into the arena to be killed by furious lions.

During Caligula's reign, he allowed the wealthy Romans to own slaves. Most of the time these slaves were treated badly. One such slave was Androcles. His owner beat him often, forced him to work long hours in the hot sun, and fed him very little food. One day, he escaped from his owner. He walked for days and found a cave to live in. Androcles knew if he was ever found, he would surely be fed to the lions!

One day while resting in his cave, he noticed a large lion at the entrance. The lion limped towards Androcles. He could tell the lion was in great pain when it lifted a sore paw as if to say, "Please help me." Androcles saw a large splinter in the lion's foot and he removed it. The grateful lion then laid down and fell asleep next to him. The two of them became close friends as they would hunt, travel, and rest together. Androcles called the lion Red Beard, because of a bright patch of fur on his chin. They lived together for three years, until Androcles was captured by the emperor's men.

He was dragged back to Rome and placed in a small jail cell. He knew he would be killed soon. Several weeks went by until the morning he was forced to go to the Colosseum. When he entered, he saw several thousand spectators cheering and waiting for him to be killed by a lion.

As he stood in the center of the arena, a very large lion was released. Often such lions were starved for days so they would be hungry and aggressive when they saw the prisoners. But something strange happened. When the lion saw Androcles, he did not attack. Instead, he stood still and studied the man. Then he slowly approached. He wagged his tail like a pet dog, came close to the terrified Androcles, and then started to gently lick him around the face and feet. Androcles now recognized the lion as his old friend Red Beard. The old friends hugged each other.

Caligula could not believe what he saw. "Why didn't the lion attack?" The emperor later talked with Androcles, who told him how he and the lion lived together for three years before he was recaptured. In a rare act of kindness, the emperor decided to set Androcles and the lion free.

People and animals can develop strong, loyal, trusting relationships

ACTIVITY 4:
A Special Bond: Man and Animal

Directions: Throughout history there has been a special bond between humans and animals. Androcles and the lion formed a close, trusting relationship. Even today most homes have pets ranging from dogs and cats to snakes and lizards. One of the more interesting times in the history of our country was the Civil War. Author and researcher Webb Garrison has written several books about the Civil War and he found that many different animals played an important role during this time period. Listed here are some of those animals that played a valuable role in US history. After studying this list of critters, gather in a small group and take turns sharing stories about close bonds you've had with animals.

Civil War Critters*

Horses: Thousands of horses were killed in battle. One soldier, General Nathan Bedford Forrest, claimed that thirty-nine horses died while he was in the saddle. Veteran US cavalrymen learned how to get extra information from their scouts, "By the nervous twitching of our horses' ears we learned that the enemy was near."

Dogs: Next to the horse, the dog was the most common animal found in the war. One soldier trained his dog to perform military salutes. General Robert E. Lee had a dog that went with him to his office every morning and stayed with him from 8:00am to 4:00pm.

Squirrels: These comical animals allowed soldiers to relax and laugh once in a while. One adopted squirrel was trained to dance as his master played the drums.

Badgers: Several Wisconsin soldiers had badgers as mascots.

Pelicans: One Louisiana regiment took a pelican to war.

Camels: One Mississippi regiment actually secured a camel to carry supplies.

Chickens: One Confederate troop trained a rooster to crow when the Federals launched an attack. Some soldiers of the Army of Northern Virginia thought the most unusual animal that took part in the conflict was a barnyard hen. The fowl became so attached to General Lee that she followed him for weeks. Making her nest under his cot, she faithfully laid an egg every morning.

Birds: Many soldiers adopted birds as mascots. The most popular were pigeons, crows, and eagles.

Bears: Officers of a Minnesota outfit bragged to comrades that their mascot was a bear that had been wounded several times before being sent home in good condition.

Describe a special bond you had with an animal:

____

____

____

* From the book, Civil War Curiosities, by Webb Garrison, 1994, Rutledge Press, Nashville.

The 59¢ Glider

At least once a week, I like to leave my counseling office and sit on a bench and watch the students play. One day, I noticed that Jason, a fourth grader, was playing by himself. He was tossing a light, balsawood glider in the air. He would throw it, chase after it, and throw it again. Jason, normally a rather quiet boy, was giggling and laughing. I had never seen him so happy.

The playground was getting crowded, as more students headed outside to play. Jason's glider flew through the air and landed near a group of fifth graders. One of them had accidentally stepped on it, crushing it. Jason ran over to the broken plane, picked it up, and started crying. I continued to watch as this rather large boy kept crying louder and louder. He was drawing a lot of attention from the others.

Soon, several older students started making comments like, "Stop crying you baby," and "What's the problem? It's only a cheap toy. You can get another one at Wal-Mart for 59¢!" Other students pointed at him and laughed. I tried to let Jason handle the problem himself, but the laughing and teasing got worse. I put my arm around him and led him to my office.

After fifteen more minutes of crying, he finally settled down. I was interested in finding out why this 10-year-old was so upset over such a small thing. He told me the following story:

"Mr. Carr, my dad left my mom before I was born. I've never seen him or talked to him. I don't even know where he lives. He never writes or sends me anything. Yesterday was my birthday and I got a card in the mail. It was from my dad, and inside the envelope was the glider. That was the first thing I ever got from him. I know it's only a cheap toy, but it came from MY dad!"

There will be times in your life when you see others getting upset over things that you think are silly or unimportant. Be careful not to judge them or overreact to their actions. You won't know the whole story. To you, a broken 59¢ glider may be nothing to get all excited about, but to Jason, it was a very sad and hurtful event.

Don't be too quick to judge others and their actions.

ACTIVITY 5:
Going Backpacking

Directions: Let's say you and a group of friends were going hiking for the weekend. All your food and necessary clothing will be taken care of so you won't have to worry about putting those items in your backpack. For your three day trip, which ten items would you take with you? Jason would have packed his glider if it hadn't been crushed. List your ten items and why you selected them. Now share your list with others.

Items	**Why?**
1. ______________	______________
2. ______________	______________
3. ______________	______________
4. ______________	______________
5. ______________	______________
6. ______________	______________
7. ______________	______________
8. ______________	______________
9. ______________	______________
10. ______________	______________

A Story of Determination

Ed and Donna were very excited. They were awaiting the birth of their first child. Not only was Donna going to deliver any day, so was the neighbor's dog. On April 17th, Donna went to the hospital to give birth to a baby boy, Danny. On the same day, Ginger, the neighbor's dog, had six puppies. Ed and Donna decided to get one of the puppies and name it Bailey. They enjoyed watching Bailey and Danny grow, and it was easy to remember their birthdays!

Danny and Bailey became close friends. They played together and slept together. When Danny went to school, Bailey would always wait at the end of the driveway until he got off the bus. They also celebrated their birthdays together. Danny would invite his friends to the parties, and Bailey had a few dog visitors as well.

As Bailey got a little older, it became difficult for her to climb the steep stairway to Danny's bedroom. Whenever Danny headed up the stairs, Bailey was right behind, although it took longer than it used to when she was a puppy. Most nights, Bailey would sleep at the foot of Danny's bed, and at times, Bailey would sleep in Ed and Donna's room.

When Bailey reached 13-years-old, she was too old and weak to climb the stairs. Danny would place Bailey's blanket at the foot of the stairs, and there she would sleep until Danny came down in the mornings. Ed and Donna began to worry. They knew Bailey was going to die soon. How would Danny handle it? Ed and Donna feared the day when Bailey would die.

Danny was beginning to realize that Bailey was weak and ill. Not only couldn't she climb stairs, she could barely walk. Danny had to carry her outside twice a day. One evening in late October, Danny picked her up and placed her on the blanket at the foot of the stairs. He patted her on the head and went upstairs to bed.

At two o'clock in the morning, Danny was awakened. He heard the sound of small feet coming up the stairs. Who or what could it be? Then he heard the sound on the floor of his room. It was Bailey. She placed her paws on the pillow next to him and licked his face. Then she left his room and went into his parents' room. Bailey went to Donna's side of the bed and kissed her, and then she went to the other side of the bed and licked Ed's face. Danny could hear Bailey's little feet hit the steps of the stairway, as she headed back down. Danny could not believe what had happened. Was he dreaming? How could the weak and crippled dog climb those stairs?

The next morning, Danny rushed down the stairs as usual to say good morning to Bailey. When he reached her blanket, he found her dead. She had died during the night.

Somehow Bailey knew she was going to die, and somehow she gathered enough strength to climb the stairs one more time to kiss her family goodbye. Bailey was determined to climb the stairs and she did it. Determination is a very important skill to master. When you wish to accomplish something, are you determined to reach your goal, or do you let excuses get in the way? Bailey knew she could reach her goal. Are you determined to reach yours?

When you are determined to reach a goal, you usually succeed at reaching it.

ACTIVITY 6:
Alphabet Soup

Directions: Have you ever started working on a problem, puzzle, or brain teaser and said, "I'm not quitting until I get it right." You were determined to succeed. Try successfully completing this problem-solving activity. All your answers will be letter of the alphabet.

---

1. What is the only letter open on all sides? ______________________

2. What are the capital letters that are the same upside down? ______________________

3. What are the capital letters containing one single horizontal line? ______________________

4. What are the capital letters with two parallel horizontal lines? ______________________

5. What are the capital letters with two diagonal straight lines? ______________________

6. Abecedarians who mind their P's & Q's should have little trouble with these questions. What letters of the alphabet are?

   a. a bird? ______________________

   b. part of your head? ______________________

   c. an insect? ______________________

   d. a drink? ______________________

   e. a building extension? ______________________

   f. a game stick? ______________________

   g. a vegetable? ______________________

   h. a body of water? ______________________

   i. a farm animal? ______________________

Shawn's Message... "Never Give Up!"

For several years in a row, I had been invited to be the keynote speaker at the fifth grade graduation ceremony at Cameron Park Elementary School in Hillsborough, North Carolina. Again, in 1997, I was asked to speak, but I thought it was time to bring in a truly motivational person to address the students and parents. So, I invited Shawn Hessee. Shawn was a senior in high school in 1997, and since he would be graduating soon, I thought the time was perfect to have him speak to our graduating fifth graders, before he moved away. When I called him, as usual, he said, "Yes, I would love to!"

Shawn Hessee is a remarkable young man who has won numerous awards and honors. He has always done well academically, and he is a very active person. He traveled the states playing basketball, he wrestled for several years, and he was one of the privileged few who got to carry the Olympic Torch on its way to the Summer Olympics in Atlanta in 1996. In 1995, he won the Athlete of the Year Award at the North Carolina State Games. In wrestling, he lettered twice and won awards for "Most Dedicated Wrestler," and "The Heart and Desire Award." He has won several trophies in Tae Kwon Do, and in his senior year of high school, he received the "Most Outstanding Person Award," by North Carolina School Student Government.

Shawn's favorite sport is wrestling. He wrestled for five years, and he was a major part of the high school's 1996-97 team that advanced to the state finals. He practiced hard every day with fellow team members, as their coaches pushed them to do their best. He rarely missed practice, and he constantly cheered and supported other wrestlers.

Wrestling coach, Bobby Shriner, says this about Shawn: "He is one of the most inspirational people I have ever met. As Shawn's wrestling coach at Orange High School, I had the privilege of watching what a total team player is all about. He never backed down to a challenge, always gave his best — both in practice and during the match, and he was the team motivator. He may not have had the same physical ability as his opponents, but he probably had more heart and determination than anyone he grappled with. At the end of each match, he had given his all - and as we say in wrestling, he "left it on the mat." Shriner goes on to say, "Shawn's inspiration upon me is unbelievable. Without knowing it, he gave me courage to push everyone else just a little bit harder in practice each day, at the same time challenging myself to strive for excellence in my own life, and in coaching."

On the evening of June 3, 1997, Shawn gave a fantastic, highly emotional speech to the students and parents that were packed into the gymnasium. He encouraged the rising middle-schoolers to never quit, to always listen to their parents, and to set goals. He also reminded them not to let others judge them on their won-loss records in sports, or by what they can or cannot do. Shawn told them that what really counts is working hard and being a good citizen. By the end of the program, many people had tears in their eyes, and the crowd gave him a standing ovation. He had accomplished what I wanted him to do — inspire and motivate.

There is more to this story…I need to tell you a few more things about Shawn Hessee. He was born three months premature. His lungs had not fully developed, which resulted in a lack of oxygen to the part of the brain that affects motor skills. Shawn has cerebral palsy. Throughout his life, he has been confined to wheelchairs, walkers, and crutches. In spite of this early setback, he has accomplished so much. One of his proudest feats centers on his wrestling career. He had 88 wrestling matches in high school. Do you know many he won? None! He lost every one! Coach Shriner adds, "Shawn may not have won any matches during his career at Orange High School, but his inspiration for all would make him a world champion on anyone's team." Thanks Shawn!

ACTIVITY 7: Shawn's Credo

Directions: Shawn's story is a great motivator. Make a copy of his "Credo" and post it in your room or on your desk as a reminder to do your best. A credo is a set of your beliefs and advice for others. What is your credo? Develop your own credo and list it below.

Shawn Hessee's Credo

1. NEVER, NEVER GIVE UP!
2. Don't judge success by your wins and losses.
3. The only way you ever really lose is when you quit.
4. Don't let what others say about you get you down.
5. True happiness comes from within and not from the approval of others.
6. Success is not always winning.
7. Don't think you failed just because things didn't work out the way you hoped; keep trying.

My name______________________________ **Date** ____________

My Credo:

1. ____

2. ____

3. ____

4. ____

5. ____

Mind Games I

Have you ever been in a situation where you did something that you normally wouldn't do, but you "went along with the crowd?" Have you ever been afraid or hesitant to be the only person in a class or group to be different? Are you willing to take a stand and do what is right, instead of doing what everyone else in the group is doing? Look over the five events that follow. Have any of these things happened to you? What would you do?

1. You are in the school cafeteria eating a sandwich and drinking a carton of milk. The milk tastes good. Then you notice a student complaining to the cafeteria manager that, "This milk is sour!" Does your milk now taste a little funny? Do you complain?

2. Students in your science class pass around a note. The note informs all students to drop a book on the floor at the same time — 1:15. When 1:15 comes, what do you do? Do you drop your book just like everyone else, or not?

3. A friend of yours asks you to sign a petition. You don't agree with the demands of the petition, but you notice that all your best friends have signed it. What do you do?

4. The teacher leaves the room for a few minutes. The other students in the class open their textbooks and cheat on the test. What do you do?

5. You find out your math teacher is Mr. Mayo. All your friends tell you that he is mean. Do you enter his class with a bad feeling knowing he is mean, or do you ignore your friends' comments and give the teacher a chance to prove differently?

All through life you are going to have to deal with difficult situations in which you have to make a decision. Do you stick to your belief system, or do you let your peers control your actions? So called "peer pressure" is not easy to deal with, and often you don't want to be seen as different, but there comes a time when you need to do what you think is right, not what the crowd thinks. Who should control your mind and your thinking — you or your peers?

Let me share the following story with you that shows how powerful peer pressure or peer influence can be. Several years ago, Alexandria was the president of the school's Student Council. She was one of the most popular students at the school. I asked her to help me with an experiment to see how much influence she had on her peers.

For the annual fund raiser, Alexandria and I, the student council advisor, decided to sell chocolate candy. First, we met with over one hundred fourth graders. Before giving each student a sample of the candy, Alexandria was told to say the following: "Here is a sample of the chocolate candy we will be selling for this year's fund raiser.

I've had several pieces and it tastes great. I think we'll be able to sell hundreds of boxes. Take a bite and then let's vote to see if we should place an order."

Next, we met with over a hundred fifth graders. Before passing out samples to the fifth graders, Alexandria was told to say the following: "Here is a sample of the chocolate candy that we will be selling for this year's fund raiser. I had one piece to eat and thought it was yucky. Go ahead and have a taste and then we will have a vote to decide if we should place an order."

I bet you can guess what happened. Over 90% of the fourth graders thought the candy tasted good. Only 22% of the fifth graders thought the candy was good. Did Alexandria's comments influence her peers?

Do what you think is right. Don't let others decide for you. Take a stand; be different if you have to. Don't forget that many years ago, a woman named Rosa Parks took a stand. Unlike many African Americans before her, she refused to sit in the back of a public bus. Because of her action, many segregation laws were changed all over the South.

Be your own person. Don't let your peers/friends "control" your emotions.

ACTIVITY 8:
School Stressors

Directions: Going to school is not always easy. Besides your schoolwork you have to cope with many peer issues that can cause you much stress. Sometimes I don't think parents/guardians are aware of all the difficult issues that young people have to deal with in school. Share the following paragraph with your parents/guardians. They may be able to give you some good advice on how to handle some of the stressors. Don't forget, they had to go through school themselves! After reviewing the stressors mentioned below, think of five major stressors that students have today that parents probably didn't have twenty years ago.

Susan Jones Sears and Joanne Milburn wrote a book entitled, *Childhood Stress*. Here is what they and other researchers found concerning school-age stressors.

According to researchers, the most common stressors of school-aged children include anxiety about going to school, bullies, changing schools, conflicts with the teacher, forced competitiveness, difficulty with classmates, fads, dares with classmates, failing exams or getting failing grades, failing to make an athletic team, having to give oral reports in front of the class, learning disorders, being unable to complete homework assignments, lack of parental interest in achievements, parental pressure to achieve, dealing with the reputation of older siblings (good or bad), worrying about taking a test, and even special recognition (for making the honor roll, winning a debate, and so on). A significant amount of stress stems from bullying, cyber-bullying, peer teasing—about being overweight, being a different race, wearing glasses, having red hair, wearing dental braces, and so on.

Ten school stressors students have today that parents probably didn't have twenty years ago:

1. ______________________
2. ______________________
3. ______________________
4. ______________________
5. ______________________
6. ______________________
7. ______________________
8. ______________________
9. ______________________
10. ______________________

Mind Games II

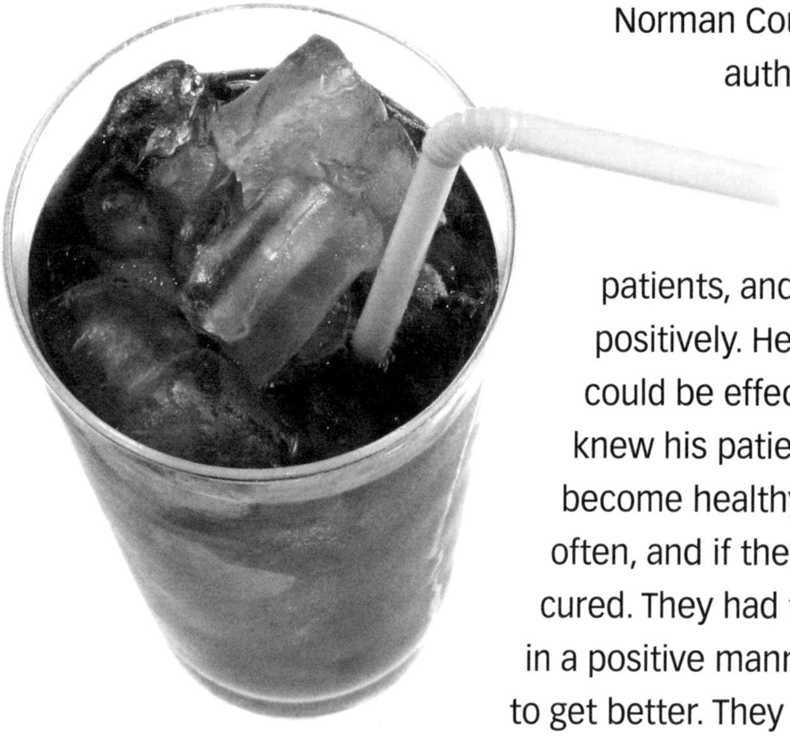

Norman Cousins was a famous doctor and author. He believed that the mind was a powerful instrument in the healing process. Cousins worked with his patients, and encouraged them to think positively. He believed that hope and humor could be effective in curing some illnesses. He knew his patients had a better chance to become healthy again, if they would laugh more often, and if they truly believed they would be cured. They had to focus their mind and thoughts in a positive manner. His patients were expected to get better. They did not solely rely on medicine.

One of his favorite stories about the power of hope and expectations involves the chain of events that happened at a high school football game in Monterey Park, California. Apparently, a few people left their seats in the stadium because they felt ill. The doctor in attendance examined their activities during the previous few hours, and concluded that all had become sick and queasy after drinking the cola that was being served at the game. The doctor then asked that a public announcement be made informing people of the possible cola contamination, and asking that no one drink any cola beverage.

Amazingly, almost 200 people in the stadium become instantly ill, and had to be hospitalized. These were people who had been fine, and who had felt no symptoms until the warning sounded over the public announcement system. The severity of symptoms and the suddenness with which they struck amazed everyone, especially the doctors at the area hospital.

A sample of the cola beverage was immediately obtained, and in the next few hours was analyzed for possible contamination. Based on the results of sophisticated tests, health officials stated that the cola was completely free of contamination and could not be the cause of everyone's illness.

The 200 desperately ill people in the local hospital suddenly and miraculously recovered, as soon as they heard that nothing was wrong with the cola. Those who had been writhing in pain only minutes before walked out of the hospital symptom-free.

Think positively! If you think you can get rid of an illness and feel better, then you have a better chance. Remember…"Ya Gotta Believe!"

ACTIVITY 9: Miracles Come in Cans

Directions: I am an optimist. I truly believe that people can accomplish great things if they really try. People can even create miracles if they use the word "can". For example, "I can study harder every day. I can start saving money today. I can practice swimming three times a week. I can choose to ignore others who tease me." Complete the following.

My goal or miracle is: ______________________________

____

Here are several things I can do to help achieve my goal:

I can: ______________________________

I can: ______________________________

I can: ______________________________

I can: ______________________________

I can: ______________________________

I can: ______________________________

The Snake and the Cowboy

Several years ago, I stopped at a 24-hour gas station in upstate New York. It was about 3:00 am and a very old man helped me pump my gas. When I went into the station to pay, he gave me a cup of coffee, and then told me a fascinating story about the Diamondback Rattlesnake. I don't know if it is true, but I enjoy telling it to others. I did learn one lesson from the tale. Sometimes in life we encounter problems, and spend many hours trying to solve them, but quite often the solutions are very simple. In fact, the answer may be right in front of our nose. You'll understand what I mean after reading this story.

Around 1850, Larry was traveling with several other cowboys, as they herded cattle through the Southwest. On one hot summer night, it was Larry's turn to stay up all night long to keep an eye on the cattle. While the others slept, Larry leaned against a tree under the stars, with a rifle in hand.

It was a peaceful night until the horses starting getting restless and making sounds around dawn. One large horse was really nervous. Larry moved in to see what the problem was. As he neared the horse, a huge Diamondback Rattlesnake struck. It bit him through his boot, it's fangs dropped venom in his veins and the snake was stuck to his boot. Several other cowboys rushed to help him. One man shot the snake with his rifle, but the snake remained attached to the boot. Two cowboys had to pull with all their strength to remove the snake!

Larry started getting weak and pale. Someone threw him over the back of a horse, and rode several hours until they found a doctor. Once inside the doctor's office, Larry took off his hat and boots. The doctor located the marks on his leg where the fangs struck.

Larry stayed at the doctor's office for several days, until he was healthy enough to ride away. Larry grabbed his hat and put his boots back on. Before leaving, the doctor told Larry that he was lucky to survive such a nasty bite. The doctor also told Larry to relax and stay indoors for a week or two, before returning to work.

Larry rode back to camp. He no sooner got there, when he started to get sick. He felt the same way he felt a few days ago when he was bitten. He was pale, shaking, and vomiting. He rushed back to the doctor who had him lie down and take off his boots. Sure enough, there was another set of fang marks on the same leg. "You've been bitten again by a rattler. I told you to rest and stay indoors!" Larry told the doctor that he did follow orders and never saw another snake.

Luckily the doctor saved Larry's life again, and he gave him another lecture before leaving. "You are a lucky man to survive two rattlesnake bites. A third bite may kill you. Stay indoors and rest." As Larry put his hat and boots on, he again told the doctor that he had not seen another snake. Out the door Larry went.

Larry was only a few miles out of town when it happened again. He got the shakes, started getting a fever, and then vomited. He turned his horse back towards town. He barely made it into the doctor's office and passed out on the floor. The doctor removed Larry's boots, and sure enough, more fang marks! "You've been bit again," said the doctor. Larry tried to convince him that he never saw a snake, but how could he argue; there were more marks on the same leg as the first two bites. Both Larry and the doctor were confused. What is happening?

Somehow, Larry survived again. This time the doctor didn't lecture to him. Instead he said, "If you get bit again, don't come to me. I'm not helping you anymore. You don't listen to me." Larry didn't say anything. He grabbed one of his boots and started to put it on when the doctor yelled, "Stop. Let me see that boot!" The doctor looked closely at the boot and shouted "Amazing!" He had found the answer to this crazy situation. There were two fangs still stuck in the boot! Apparently, when the cowboys pulled the snake off Larry's boot, the fangs remained stuck inside. So every time Larry put his boots back on, the fangs scratched his leg, causing it to bleed, and allowing a small amount of venom to enter his system. The doctor took out a pair of pliers and removed the fangs. Problem solved!

The solution to many problems is easier than we think.

Directions: Are you good at thinking of simple ways to solve difficult problems that you encounter almost daily? Remember, most solutions to problems are easier than you think. Designer Scott Love gives us some "food for thought" for seeing the "obvious" in most problems, "Only the most foolish of mice would hide in a cat's ear, but only the wisest of cats would think to look there."

Try this one.

You can see a large delivery truck that has become stuck beneath an underpass because it is one inch too tall to fit under. The driver has a load of melting ice cream that he needs to get to the grocery store as soon as possible. The truck is stuck and can't back up. There are no other roads leading to the store. Do you have a simple solution to this dilemma? How can the truck get through the underpass?

Try these puzzlers.
Adapted from ***So You Think You're Smart*** by Pat Battaglia.

A hint to each of twelve words is given below. Each of the twelve words rhymes with a name of an animal. Determine the twelve animals. Answers are in the back of the book.

Example: present time *Answer: cow (rhymes with now)*

1. a ground cloud
2. glove
3. an alcoholic beverage
4. hockey disk
5. above 98.6 degrees
6. ballot
7. a two-digit number
8. a running-track barrier
9. rough or abrasive
10. prison
11. person in monastery
12. cogitate

A Great Nurse

The bell rang at 2:45 as usual, and Emily grabbed her bookbag and rushed outside the high school. Just like most days, a rude classmate shouted, "Hey Emily, you going to visit Henrietta Hunchback again?" Robbie followed with, "You don't need to feed that old lady, come with us to the skating rink." Her friends just didn't understand. She ran home, threw her books on the floor, put some fruit in a bag, and started the one mile walk to Henrietta's place.

Henrietta, who was 85-years-old, lived by herself in a rented shack just outside of town. Several years ago, her husband died in a fire that destroyed their home. The fire left her badly burned, her face with many scars, and her body deformed with a large bump or hunch on her back. She could barely walk, and seldom had money for food. Emily visited her almost every day. She would bring her food, straighten up the house, water Henrietta's plants, and feed her cat.

The one thing Henrietta looked forward to the most was the long talks she and Emily would have. Emily would read to her and then they would talk for hours. Henrietta was always excited to hear Emily talk about wanting to be a nurse. Henrietta encouraged Emily to study hard and keep praying, and maybe one day she would be able to go to college. Emily had her doubts, because she knew her father could not afford to send her off to college.

One January, a typical Nebraska blizzard hit the area. Roads and schools were closed for days. Emily worried about Henrietta. Did she have enough food to eat, and was there enough wood for the fireplace? Her Dad was finally able to get out to buy some much needed food for Emily and himself. When he returned with several bags of groceries, Emily met him at the door. She could read his face and knew something was wrong. He gave her the bad news. "Emily, John at the store told me that Henrietta died yesterday. I'm sorry."

Even though Henrietta died, Emily continued to visit her shack. She still watered the plants and fed the cat. She missed her old friend.

About four months later, Emily's father stopped by the school early to pick her up. This was very unusual. "Emily, I just found out that we have to be at a very important meeting at the courthouse." When they arrived, they were ushered to an office where several men were sitting. A town lawyer, Mr. Williamson, began to read an important document, "I, Henrietta Hansen, being of sound mind and body hereby command the following. Because of her love, caring, and compassion, and because she wishes to be a nurse, and because I know she will be a great one; I leave Emily Lewis all my life savings of $53,250 to be used to pay her college tuition. God Bless You, Emily."

After the lawyers read Henrietta's will, Emily hugged her Dad and tears came to her eyes. Emily did go to college, got her degree, became a nurse, and was a great one!

"You can get everything in life you want if you help enough other people get what they want."
— Zig Ziglar

ACTIVITY 11:
Random Acts of Kindness

Directions: One cold January morning I stopped by the post office. In the parking lot I found a letter. I picked it up and noticed that it was someone's power/electric envelope but no stamp was attached. Obviously someone was going to purchase a stamp and mail the bill but, they dropped it. I went inside, put a stamp on it and dropped it in the mail. Later I thought, "What if I hadn't mailed the bill to the power company?" Would the power company cut off electricity to the family? Were there kids in the family who might have gone without heat? Would the power company believe the person when he/she claimed that they did mail the bill? Would the person's credit rating be lowered? "Many bad things" could have happened if I hadn't mailed the lost letter. I considered actions such as this as a random act of kindness; I didn't have to do it but I did. If I had dropped a bill on the ground, I would hope someone would do the same for me. We need to help others even if no one else knows it. The person who lost his power bill will never know what I did. Following are ten examples of "acts of kindness." Check at least three you promise to do this week.

Random Acts of Kindness

- ☐ **Do some work around the house without being told**
- ☐ **Pick up litter in your neighborhood**
- ☐ **Volunteer to read stories for students in the lower grades**
- ☐ **Take a neighbor's dog for a walk**
- ☐ **Mow your neighbor's grass**
- ☐ **Without getting caught, place a candy bar on your teacher's desk**
- ☐ **Bake some cookies for a relative**
- ☐ **Shovel snow off the sidewalks**
- ☐ **Give part of your allowance to charity**
- ☐ **Put some seeds out for the birds**
- ☐ **Other act (s)** ______________________________

____

What's in your pocket?

There is a television commercial by a major credit card company that ends with their spokesperson asking viewers, "What's in your wallet?" The company tries to convince people that their credit is the best. For this story I'm not going to ask, "What's in your wallet?" Instead I'm asking, "What's in your pocket?" Yes, most of us carry several tangible items in our pockets such as keys, gum, tissues, loose change and perhaps a few dollars. But I believe we are carrying a few other 'invisible' things with us. In your pockets are you carrying around positive character traits like compassion, forgiveness, kindness, and integrity? Or are you guilty of filling your pockets with anger, revenge, blame, guilt, and making excuses? What's in your pocket? I'll return to these questions at the end of this story.

Have you ever slipped on a pair of jeans you hadn't worn in a while and reached into a pocket and found some money that you didn't know was there? Wow! What a great feeling. On the other hand, have you ever stepped up to the cash register in the cafeteria or convenience store and reached into your pocket to get your money and it wasn't there? How embarrassing! Do you get angry and ask yourself, "Who stole my money?" Do you wonder who picked your pocket?

I'm sure you've heard about pickpockets, people who take things from other people's pockets. They are sneaky, crafty and seldom get caught. Pickpockets have been around for years, especially in large European cities like London. I am sure many of your remember the story Oliver Twist that was written by Charles Dickens. It took place in London in the early 1800's and tells the plight of an orphan named Oliver Twist who joined a gang of pickpockets. He mastered this skill as a means of survival.

Over the years the city of London has tried numerous strategies to combat pickpockets. They put up signs warning tourists to 'keep their eyes open' and guard their valuables. Many years ago there was a judge who got so frustrated dealing with the numerous pickpockets that entered his court room that he came up with a clever punishment. Men or women who were found guilty of this crime were ordered to wear boxing gloves whenever they were in the streets. It is very difficult to pick pockets with boxing gloves on your hands! If any of these thieves were caught without their gloves during their probation time, they were sent to jail. Just recently a broadband provider in London known as 'Talk Talk' came up with a unique idea to improve the image of London streets. This group came up with an idea called, "Put-Pocketing." Men and women travel the streets and secretly put money into people's pockets without them noticing. These specially trained men and women are not 'pick-pocketing,' they are 'put-pocketing.' In fact, the Put-Pocketing teams include several ex-pickpockets. One former pickpocket said that it felt good to give something back for a change and he also stated that every time he put money in someone's pocket he felt less guilty about all the times he stole from others. Signs along the street note, "Rejoice! Put-Pockets operating in this area."

Lucy Morgan Beard was a school teacher in North Carolina in the late 1800's. She was known for her honesty, fair play, and willingness to go out of the way to help others. She carried several positive character traits in her pocket. One year she traveled to London. She desired to see a section of the city noted for its rough element, pickpockets and crime. She had been advised not to go there but took the risk. She tucked her pocketbook in her stocking. As she walked along the street, a young man stepped up behind her and said, "Lady, you dropped this." Being wary, she told him in no uncertain terms to keep his distance. She thought he was trying to distract her so he could steal something from her. Then she recognized her pocketbook. She had dropped it and he was returning it. She was so grateful to him and felt so bad for being rude to the young man that she sent him money every month as long as she lived and left a small sum to him when she died.

What's in your pocket? Do you carry around the traits of revenge or forgiveness? If someone stole money from your jacket, can you forgive them? Sure, you can report it and never forget what they did, but you'll never be totally comfortable with yourself until you learn to forgive.

Practice being creative.

ACTIVITY 12:
Pebbles in Pockets

Directions: Are you having trouble getting along with someone? Remember, you can't change that person, but if you change, that person might. Get your creative mind in gear. Come up with a five step plan of action. List five things that you will do that will help the two of you get along better.

When I was in elementary school I had a difficult time getting along with a boy in my class named Timothy. He enjoyed calling me a "Pea Brain." No matter how much I complained to the teacher, Timothy kept teasing me. After a while I realized I couldn't change him, but I could change how I interacted with him. I had to get creative. I sat down with a pencil and paper and drew up a plan. Here was my plan:

1. I stopped tattling on him.
2. I invited him whenever I could to be on my team, to sit with me at lunch, or to work on a project.
3. I agreed to 'stick up' for him when others bothered him.
4. I found something we had in common. We both loved trading baseball cards.
5. Every morning I would put three pebbles in my left pocket. Whenever I said something nice to him I would move one pebble from my left pocket to my right. At the end of the day, after I said three nice things to him, all three pebbles would end up in the right pocket. The pebbles were great reminders!

Timothy and I ended up being good friends.

______________________________**'s Creative Plan of Action:**

YOUR NAME HERE

1. ______________________________

2. ______________________________

3. ______________________________

4. ______________________________

5. ______________________________

Mistakes

DID YOU KNOW?

- Hank Aaron and Babe Ruth are the two greatest home run hitters ever, but they both struck out more often than 99.9% of the men who ever played.
- Richard Petty won more NASCAR races than anyone, but he also lost more races than anyone.
- Pete Rose had more base hits than any player ever in major league baseball history, but he also got out more than anyone.
- Thomas Edison failed on over 14,000 experiments/attempts before finally inventing the light bulb.
- Ty Cobb held the major league record for stealing bases in a career, but he also got caught stealing more than anyone in baseball history.
- Dr. Seuss and Alex Haley had hundreds of rejections between them when trying to get their books published. They both eventually succeeded and became two of the most famous authors in our country.
- Wilt Chamberlain is the only man in NBA history to score 100 points in a game. He led the league in scoring several years in a row. Although most people don't know it, Wilt was one of the worst foul shooters ever to play the game.

Are these people known today because of their mistakes/failures, or for their successes? When you mention the name Richard Petty, do people say, "Oh, he's the guy who lost the most races," or do they say, "He's the man who won the most NASCAR races?" When people hear Edison's name, do they say, "He's the scientist who failed over 14,000 times on one invention," or do people say, "He's the man who invented the light bulb?" Most people are remembered for their successes, not their mistakes or failures. Successful people did not become well-known overnight. Along their way, they made numerous mistakes.

Let's take a close look at one of the greatest athletes of all time — Michael Jordan. See if you can correctly answer this question about him:

> During Michael Jordan's career in the NBA, what percent of his shots (field goals) did he make? This includes all shots except free throws.
> a) 89%
> b) 93%
> c) 49%
> d) 68%

The correct answer is C. Yes, during his long NBA career he made only 49% of his shots. He missed more than he made. Note: he was an excellent free-throw shooter making 85% from the free-throw line. So, here is another famous person who made as many mistakes (missed field goals), as he had successes (made field goals). He was not afraid to take shots, and he lived for those pressure moments in a tight ball game. Who else would you want to take a shot at the basket in the last seconds of a tie game?

Don't be afraid to make mistakes. The difference between successful and unsuccessful people is that successful people learn from their mistakes and they keep trying and trying until they achieve their goals. Abe Lincoln, for instance, ran for political offices at least a dozen times and lost each election until he finally won one, the Presidency of the United States!

It's O.K. to make mistakes — as long as you learn from them.

ACTIVITY 13: Learning From Our Mistakes

Directions: Here are two quotes about "mistakes." Read each one then write a short paragraph about what you think each one means. Then share your responses with others.

1. **"Mistakes are often the best teachers."** — J.A. Froude

2. **"The man who makes no mistakes does not usually make anything."** — W.C. Magee

If Tomorrow Never Comes

Several years ago singer Garth Brooks had a big hit song entitled, "If Tomorrow Never Comes." In the song, he reminds us to tell those we care about how much they mean to us every day. Tell your parents or that someone special, "I Love You!" today, because you never know what may happen to you or them tomorrow.

Jake, who was 15-years-old, lived with his mother and his 5-year-old sister, Chrissy. Most of the time, Jake got along well with his sister. Chrissy truly loved her older brother. Since she did not know her father, she often looked up to Jake as her father. She would follow him around the house and often copy him. When he was doing his homework, she would pretend to do her math and reading. When he mowed the lawn, she was right behind him with her plastic toy mower. Jake would sit for hours in his room sorting and looking over his baseball card collection, and Chrissy would be at her little desk playing with her comic cards. The highlight of her day happened every night when Jake would read her a story before going to bed.

Jake had a terrible day at school on Monday. He failed a science test, lost his new jacket, and was accused of copying another student's homework. He was angry!

As he entered his house, he could hear some giggling and other noises coming from his room. Who was in his room? He pushed open his door. There was Chrissy at his desk with a peanut butter sandwich in one hand, and several of this valuable Nolan Ryan cards in the other. She did not realize she was doing anything wrong; she was just copying her big brother. Jake exploded, "Get out of my room this instant!" She tried to talk to him but he wouldn't listen. He added, "I hate you, and I wish you were never born!"

Jake ignored her the rest of the evening. Several times she told him she was sorry, but he did not respond. At bedtime she cried and begged him to read her a story, but he acted like he couldn't hear her. Chrissy cried herself to sleep.

Tuesday was a much better day at school for Jake. He whistled a tune as he headed for home. On his way, he began to think about Chrissy and all the unkind things he had said to her. He told himself that as soon as he got home, he would tell her he was sorry and read her a story. As he turned into the driveway, he sensed something was wrong. His mother's car was not there and his neighbor, Mrs. Collins, met him at the door.

Jake asked, "What's wrong?" Mrs. Collins told him that Chrissy had a bad fall and his mother had to rush her to the hospital. His sister was in critical condition. Jake sat on the couch, and he remembered the last words he had said to her, "I hate you and I wish you were never born!" He thought, "What if she dies?" He prayed, "Please God, let her live."

The next ten days went by slowly as Chrissy fought for her life. Jake couldn't sleep and hardly ate any food. He promised to tell her every day that he loved her if she came home. And she did!

ACTIVITY 14: Musical Messages

Directions: Can you think of some songs that have powerful messages? Use the space provided on the next page to list them.

Garth Brooks' song, "If Tomorrow Never Comes," reminds us to tell those special people in our lives that we love and care about them today because we don't know what will happen tomorrow. Many songs provide the listener with a powerful message. Here are two songs that come to mind.

1. Whitney Houston's biggest hit was, "The Greatest Love of All." The lyrics tell us that the greatest love of all is the ability to love ourselves. If we don't love ourselves then it is almost impossible to love others.
2. Michael Jackson's hit, "The Man in the Mirror," notes that if you are not happy with yourself or with all the bad things happening in the world, stop complaining and blaming others. The only person who can begin to change things to please you is the person you see when you look in the mirror.

Song ______________________________

Singer(s) ______________________________

Message ______________________________

____

____

Song ______________________________

Singer(s) ______________________________

Message ______________________________

____

____

Keep Honking

I believe that one of the most beautiful and fascinating sights in nature occurs in the spring and fall. It's when the Canada geese fly over head. You can always hear them honking as they fly in a V-formation. No matter what I'm doing, I'll stop and watch the flock zip by. What a sight!

Believe it or not, we can learn a lot from these amazing birds. First of all, they are always honking. Scientists and other animal experts believe their honking acts as support or encouragement. They honk to cheer on their members. The honking acts as a motivator.

They fly in a V-formation for a very important reason. When they fly in that special way, the flock can travel up to 75% further than a single goose flying by itself. They realize they can reach their destination quicker as a group, than by flying separately. By flying in the V-formation, each goose creates a partial vacuum for the goose that follows. This is a type of drafting that helps pull each bird along.

The lead goose has the hardest job as it fights the wind. It has no other goose blocking the wind for it. Every few miles another goose takes over the lead and the former lead goose goes to the back. If the lead goose is shot down by a hunter, another goose will take over. The geese take turns automatically; they never seem to argue or fight about it.

We need to take what we learn from the geese and apply it in our everyday life. Let's honk or cheer for our friends and classmates. Tell them they are doing a good job. Encourage them to keep going and to do their best.

Just like the geese, we all need to cooperate and work together. Everyone in the class will be more successful when they become a team-member and do their fair share of work. Remember, if you decide to fly on your own, it will take you much longer to accomplish your goal. The geese know that they will reach their goal much quicker as a group, than if they fly individually.

Just like the changing of the lead goose, we must take turns in class, and we need to take turns without a lot of arguing or fussing.

So...who are the smart ones, us or the geese? Let's work like the Canada geese and we'll all be more successful.

Learning to work in a group and getting along with others are valuable skills.

ACTIVITY 15:
Cheerleaders, Coaches, & CD's

Directions: Just as the geese are encouraged and motivated by the honking of other geese, people can be inspired by their friends and family. The people who try to get us to do our best could be called cheerleaders or coaches. Everybody finds a time in their life when they start feeling down, lazy or unmotivated and some encouraging words from a friend may boost them up. Here is an idea that you may want to use to help cheer, coach, and encourage someone else.

Let's say you have a friend named Ashley who appears to be going through some difficult times in her life. Maybe she is moving away, recently broke-up with a boyfriend, or is struggling in Algebra. She needs a boost. Get together with a few friends and bring along a blank CD and recorder. Make a recording for Ashley.

On the recording try some of these ideas:

1. **Have each friend say something positive about her.**
2. **Give her a loud two minute standing ovation with cheers.**
3. **Make up a clever cheer: "Two, four, six, eight!"<br>"Ashley, we think you're great!"**
4. **Do a section that starts, "Remember the time we..."**
5. **Sing her a funny song.**
6. **Encourage her to call whenever she wishes to talk.**
7. **Read a couple motivational quotes.**
8. **Tell a funny joke.**
9. **Tell her to be on the 'look out' for a surprise or two.**
10. **Encourage to her encourage others who also may be struggling.**

Send her the recording in a decorated box and tell her to play it whenever she needs a lift. She will always treasure the gift.

Parents and other family members can also create such a recoding to give to a son or daughter or siblings who go off to college, joins the service, or moves out of state.

499 in a Row!

Harold "Bunny" Levitt loved playing basketball, but he could never make the team because he was only 5'4" tall, he couldn't pass, couldn't dribble, and he couldn't make lay-ups or long shots. The only thing he was good at was making free throws. Even his foul shooting could be a problem at times, because other players would tease him about the way he shot the ball. He would toss the ball underhand, placing two hands on the ball. Others would laugh and yell out, "You shoot like a girl," or "Why are you shooting granny style?" He wasn't wanted on any team.

One day, Harold saw a poster advertising a basketball contest. For weeks he practiced secretly for the contest. He shot hundreds of free throws every day. He usually practiced early in the morning, or in the dark, so other boys wouldn't tease or bother him.

Many people questioned him on the day of the contest. One boy said, "What are you doing here? You can't play basketball!" Many participants gathered to watch Harold start shooting foul shots. As usual, he grabbed the ball with two hands and shot underhanded. Most everyone laughed and pointed at him, but soon the laughing stopped. Harold swished one basket after another. He made 100 in a row, 200, 300, 400, and then he missed his first shot which would have been number 500. Yes he made 499 baskets in a row!

The contest supervisor told Harold that he was the winner of the foul shooting contest. Harold would not take the prize. Instead, he returned to the free throw line and started shooting again. Hardly anyone left. People were amazed as Harold continued to make shot after shot without missing. At 2:30 in the morning, the janitor had to beg him to stop shooting so he could lock-up and go home. When he stopped, he had made another 371 in a row. For the night, he made 870 out of 871! Nobody teased Harold again.

Soon after that, Harold was invited to travel and play with the world famous Harlem Globetrotters. Also, he would travel around the country to challenge other basketball players in foul shooting contests. He offered $1,000 to any man who could beat him in a contest of 100 foul shots. He never lost. His worst performance was 96 out of 100.

Harold "Bunny" Levitt proved to many people that if you practice hard enough, you can reach your goal. What do you want to achieve? Start practicing!

You will be amazed at all the things you can accomplish if you only take time to practice.

ACTIVITY 16:
The 10,000 Rule

Directions: Complete the following questions. They will help you begin to master your talent.

It has often been noted that a person must practice at least 10,000 hours to become an expert at something, to truly master a skill. You might be saying "How can I practice that many hours?" Well, it will take many years, but it can be done! Let's say that Venus and Serena Williams, two great tennis pros, started practicing their tennis skills at the age of 8. They practiced 20 hours and week for ten years. By the time they were 18, they had their 10,000 hours and they were making a lot of money on the tennis courts.

Twenty hours a week may be a bit much for most young people, so how about ten hours a week? In ten years that will give you over 5,000 hours. Anything you do for 5,000 hours will make you good at it.

1. **What is my passion? What do I want to become very good at?**

2. **Do your math.**

   My age now________ In ten years I'll be __________

   If I practice my passion five hours a week for ten years,
   I will have practiced this many hours .... [ ]

   If I practice my passion ten hours a week for ten years,
   I will have practiced this many hours .... [ ]

   If I practice my passion fifteen hours a week for ten years,
   I will have practiced this many hours .... [ ]

   If I practice my passion twenty hours a week for ten years,
   I will have practiced this many hours .... [ ]

3. **If I practice my passion 5, 10, 15, or 20 hours a week, here are five things I will have less time to do:**

____

____

____

The Genius and the Average Student

Ralph and Shawn are sixth graders at the same school. Ralph is considered one of the smartest kids at school. His teachers and parents think he is smart, so he obviously believes he is smart. He scores 99% on almost every achievement test he takes. Other students call him a "walking encyclopedia." By some standards, he could be called a genius. Shawn is considered an average student at best. His parents and teachers call him "average." He usually gets C's on his report card.

One day, the two boys are out hiking with their scout troop and they get lost. As they near a small mountain, they look up and see a very large, furious, hungry-looking bear. They both are frightened. Ralph looks at the bear and scratches his head. Ralph, the

smart kid, says to Shawn, "That appears to be an Alaskan Brown Bear. They grow up to 9 feet tall, can weigh up to 1500 pounds, and can run up to 25 miles an hour. The bear is about 350 feet away, the angle of the hill is 27 degrees, and the wind is blowing 15 miles per hour from the southwest. I figure the bear will get to us in 18.2 seconds."

As Ralph was spouting out all this information, he looks over and sees Shawn taking off his backpack and hiking boots. The "average" kid is putting on his jogging shoes. Ralph yells, "Shawn, you can't outrun that bear!" Shawn looks at his buddy and says, "Hey, I don't have to outrun the bear, all I have to do is outrun you!"

This funny story has a serious side to it as well. Remember, Ralph was the "school-smart" boy who was filled with as much information as a computer. Shawn didn't have all the facts like Ralph, but he did have better practical sense that got him out of a dangerous situation. While in school, it is very important to learn facts, numbers, dates, formulas, theories, and memorize important things. All these are considered to create analytical intelligence. Yes, you need to have some basic skills, but what is more important is to have practical, or "common sense" intelligence. As in the case of this story, Shawn was not as intelligent with school facts as Ralph was, but he had more practical or common sense to survive the bear attack.

So keep studying and do your schoolwork, but take time to practice solving everyday problems, such as getting along with others, getting yourself out of sticky situations, and try being more creative.

To be "school-smart" is important, but you also need practical, common sense intelligence.

ACTIVITY 17: Confronting the Bear

Directions: In our story, Ralph and Shawn encounter a real bear. Ralph tries to "out-think" the bear while Shawn decides to "out-run" the bear.

With the help of your teacher, try this interesting "bear" activity with everyone in class.
1. Tell the class: "Imagine you are walking alone in the woods and you are confronted by a bear."
2. Ask each student: "Give me a one-word response as to what you would do in that situation?"
3. Teacher or leader: "I will list these words on the board or on a flip chart."

The leader then tells the class/group that the answers given are also how we respond to the "bears" we meet every day, the problems we face on a daily basis. Our daily "bears" can be difficult people, situations, or problems. The leader will begin a group discussion to look at each word and discuss the pros and cons. For example, is it best to "run" from our "bears" or confront them?

List at least three difficult situations or people that you have to confront on a regular basis. Also think of one strategy that has helped you survive the "bears."

Confronting the "BEARS" in my life.

1. The bear ______________________________

Strategy ______________________________

____

2. The bear ______________________________

Strategy ______________________________

____

3. The bear ______________________________

Strategy ______________________________

____

The Door of Opportunity

Over the years, I have read several books about Harry Houdini. He is considered by many to be the greatest escape artist ever. He has escaped from straitjackets while suspended over busy streets. He was locked in metal boxes and thrown in the river, only to swim to the surface a few minutes later. There have been hundreds of stories told about this amazing individual. I'm sure many of the stories are not true and some are exaggerated, made to be more unbelievable than they really were. The following is one of those remarkable stories.

Harry often bragged that he could escape from any jail in the world in less than an hour. He traveled the world and won thousands of dollars in bets. No jail could hold him! Once, he was invited to a small town in England, in which the mayor challenged him to see if he could escape from their new jail. Houdini accepted the challenge.

Hundreds of people gathered around the new jail cell. Houdini entered in his street clothes, and a curtain was placed over the cell so no one could see what was happening inside. Once inside, he took off his belt and pulled out a sharp instrument that had been hidden inside the lining. For well over an hour he picked at the lock. He could not get the door open. The spectators began to get excited. Had Houdini finally met his match? Could he get out?

On the inside, Houdini continued to pick the lock, and after nearly two hours, he collapsed against the door from sheer exhaustion. When he fell against the door, it opened. They had never locked the door! They tricked Houdini!

In Houdini's mind, the door was locked, but in reality it was not. The same can be said about the "door of opportunity." If you really believe you can reach your goals in life, then your door of opportunity is open. If you keep making excuses and not setting goals, then your door of opportunity is closed and locked. There is a saying that reads, "If you think you can or if you think you can't, you're right!" Go ahead and set goals, and kick that door wide open!

Your door of opportunity is either closed or open — it is up to you.

ACTIVITY 18:
What's Your AQ?

Directions: You can accomplish almost anything you want as long as you believe your door of opportunity is open. In life, everyone runs into a roadblock that may make it more difficult to pass through the door. These roadblocks are called adversities. An adversity is something negative that affects you. Samples could include: parents' divorce, death in the family, failing a grade, having to move often, having a learning problem, living in poverty, or having a serious disease or injury. Successful people overcome adversities. Unsuccessful people use their adversities as excuses.

In his book *The Adversity Quotient*, author Paul Stoltz believes that when people face adversities they become "quitters," "campers," or "climbers." Read the following descriptions of these three types of people. Place an "x" next to the type of person you believe you are when you find a roadblock in front of your door of opportunity.

- ☐ **Quitter:** When bad things happen you always blame others. Whenever you make a mistake you get angry and refuse to try again. You believe parents and teachers don't like you. When things don't work out you always come up with excuses.
- ☐ **Camper:** If you are a "camper" then you seldom try new things or take risks to improve yourself. You are content just to keep things the way they are. If you are a "C" student then you continue to do average work instead of studying harder. You seldom question people and accept things that happen to you, good or bad. You usually do just enough to get by.
- ☐ **Climber:** When bad things happen and you "fall on your face," you get back up and try again. You seldom use excuses. You set goals and strive to reach them. You realize that you are responsible for your actions. You have a desire to prove to yourself and others that you can do great things in life in spite of the occasional roadblocks.

Climbers:
Think of a time you were successful at something because you were a climber.

____

____

____

____

____

Now, share your success with others.

Animals as Teachers

Animals Make Us Laugh...
Our neighbors have a dog named Baxter. When he was young, they trained him to get the morning newspaper. When he brought the newspaper to the front door, they gave him a Milk Bone® for a treat. Baxter began to figure something out. He knew that if he brought a newspaper to the front door, he would get a treat. For the next few weeks, he traveled up and down the street stealing everybody's newspaper, and piled them up on his front porch, hoping he would get more treats. It took awhile to break him of the bad habit.

Animals Teach Us About Loyalty...
I once heard a story about an elderly man and a dog named Bobby. The old man gave food to the homeless dog, and soon they became close friends. When the man died, Bobby wouldn't leave his grave site until he died 14 years later! The only time he left the tombstone was to venture into town to find food. Bobby survived many harsh winters and hot summers to be near his old friend.

Animals Show Us How to Handle Tough Times...
In the book, *It's Always Something*, Gilda Radner tells a story about her cousin's dog. The dog was pregnant and the puppies were due any day. While the dog was in the front yard, she was run over by a lawn mower, cutting her two back legs off. The owners took her to the vet, who told them that the puppies were okay, but the mother would have to be put to sleep. The owners convinced the vet not to have the mother killed. The vet removed the puppies and sewed up her backside. The mother dog did an excellent job raising her puppies, even though she could barely walk. When she did, she would take two steps in the front and then flip her backside, take two more steps in the front, and flip her backside again. It was a funny sight. When her puppies started walking, they walked just like her!

Animals Help Us to Handle Our Emotions...

"I remember a sharp disappointment on the death of a pet rabbit. It developed a growth in the jaw and was sent to the vet to be killed. This was explained to me and I was reconciled to its loss. But the vet on his own initiative decided to operate. He sent the animal back a week later, pronouncing it cured. I greeted it ecstatically and it died that night."

— Evelyn Waugh

Animals Will Risk Their Lives for Us...

In Stephanie LaLands's book, *Peaceful Kingdom*, she writes several stories about birds, cats and dogs, awakening their owners when their houses were on fire. There was a fox terrier that barked and frantically tried to alert her sleeping owners. She jumped on them and pulled their bed covers away to let them know there was a fire. Only after rescuing the family did she return to the burning house to save her puppies.

Animals Teach us How to Trust

One of my favorite books is, *The Man Who Listens to Horses*. The author, Monty Roberts, compares the ways his father "broke" horses, to the way he did. His father would take a wild horse and prepare it to be ridden. He would tie the horses up, beat them, inflict much pain, and do everything possible to take the spirit out of the horse. It took his father three weeks to train a horse.

Monty tried to communicate with the horse. He wanted the horse to trust and respect him. While preparing a horse to be saddled, he never laid a hand on the horse. There was no hitting or humiliation. He would have the horse ready to go in less than thirty minutes. Monty shows us all that we can accomplish more through trust and respect, than with fear and punishment.

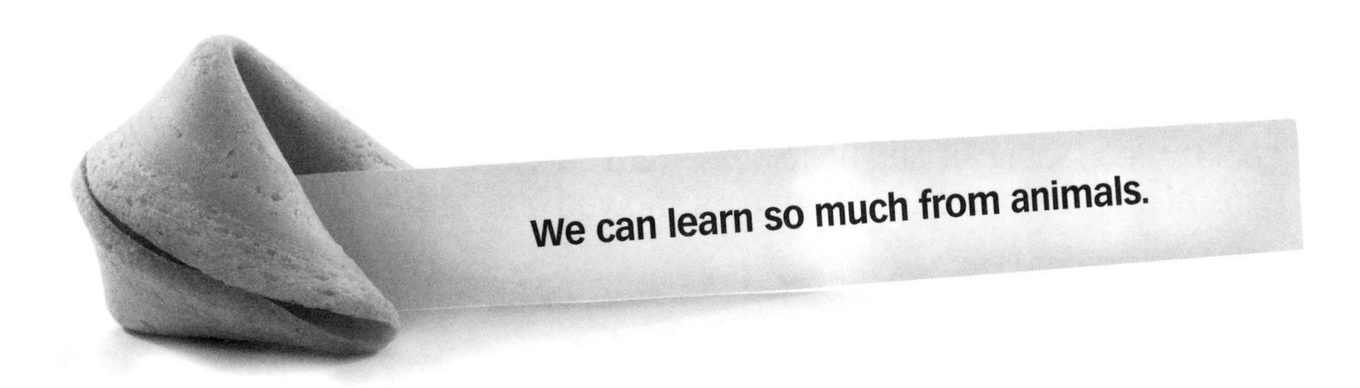

ACTIVITY 19: Animals...Animals...Animals

Directions: Answer these questions about animals. Share your answers with friends or classmates.

1. What is the funniest thing you ever saw an animal do?

2. What is the most amazing trick you ever saw an animal do?

3. Can you think of a valuable life lesson you learned from a pet?

4. Can you think of a time when you were very afraid of an animal?

5. If you could have any animal you wanted for a pet, what would you choose?

6. If you could be an animal, what would you be? Why?

7. What is your favorite television or movie animal? Why?

8. Do you think many animals share similar emotions of humans such as anger, jealousy, fear, sadness, and happiness? ❑ YES ❑ NO.
   Think of a time when one of your pets showed one of these emotions.

'Rolling Pin' Smith's Sacrifice

According to *Webster's New World Dictionary*, one of the definitions for the word **sacrifice** is, "a giving up of one thing for the sake of another." We hear the word often.

- In baseball a hitter lays down a **sacrifice** bunt. He gets out on purpose in order to advance a base runner, getting him in a better position to score on the next hit.
- Soldiers often **sacrifice** their lives for our country's freedom.
- Parents may **sacrifice** their needs to help their children.
- Some religions may encourage men or women to **sacrifice** the luxuries of modern day life to seek solitude and pray.

Throughout history there have been thousands and thousands of people who made great sacrifices to better themselves, their families, and/or their countries. In American history one of the greatest periods of sacrifice centered on the Oregon Trail era. In the late 1830's and early 1840's thousands of men, women, and children left their eastern homes and headed west looking for a better life: more jobs, better land for farming, and nicer weather. These folks often left behind friends, family members, their churches, and their homes. They loaded up their wagons and traveled west in hopes of a better life.

When we think of the Oregon Trail many of us envision mothers, fathers, and children riding in covered wagons pulled by horses or oxen. But research has discovered that almost everyone walked the 1,932 miles to Oregon. Why? There were four reasons for this: (1) there was little room to ride since the wagons were loaded with supplies; (2) the ride was very bumpy (no shock absorbers!); (3) the emigrants didn't want to add additional weight for the oxen to pull; (4) walking afforded time to socialize with acquaintances and friends along the Trail.

As the wagons moved further west the emigrants encountered many challenges: bad weather, hostile Indians, bandits, illnesses, and water and food shortages. The animals that were pulling wagons began to tire so the pioneers had to make several sacrifices. They had to decide which objects could be discarded to make the loads lighter for the animals. Along the Trail later travelers often found items that were tossed away: pianos, heavy tools, pots and pans, and pieces of furniture. Tough decisions, tough sacrifices had to be made to assist the weary animals that pulled the wagons.

On one wagon was a rugged middle-aged man named Smith. At one of the rest stops the group leader gathered his band together and told them they must toss away any unnecessary items or else the pullers couldn't progress. Each person searched their belongings. Which items could be sacrificed for the group? About the only item Smith had left was a large, heavy, wooden rolling pin. This large man began to tear-up when told to throw the heavy item aside. "Do I have to throw it away? It was my mother's.

I remember she always used it to roll out her delicious biscuits. Please, please, please let me keep it." Smith had to make a quick decision, either get rid of the rolling pin or be left behind. With tears flowing down his checks, he buried the pin in the ground. He did his fair share; he made a sacrifice. Others in his group wondered if he ever returned to that spot to retrieve his priceless item. For the rest of the journey they christened him "Rolling Pin" Smith, a name he carried to the day of his death.

We often need to make sacrifices for our self or for others.

ACTIVITY 20:
Sacrifices along the Trail

Directions: In our story 'Rolling Pin' Smith had to make a big sacrifice. He wasn't the only traveler to make a sacrifice; thousands of others did as well along the Oregon Trail. For this activity you have been selected to lead a large group of pioneers on the trip west. Besides food and other important supplies you need to select a talented group of individuals to help ensure a successful trip. Study the following list of jobs that are needed. Then rank them 1-14, with #1 being, in your opinion, the most important person, #2 the second most important person for the group, etc. When you finish, compare your list with others and discuss. In your group see if you can agree which person(s) would you sacrifice, leave behind, if you had to.

_____ **Doctor** (to help heal the sick and wounded)

_____ **Scout** (to look for good roads, passes, and to look out for Indians)

_____ **Pastor** (to lead church services and preside over funerals)

_____ **Mechanic/Blacksmith** (to shoe horses, repair wagons)

_____ **Cook** (to prepare three meals a day for the travelers)

_____ **Storyteller** (to tell stories and entertain weary travelers at night near the camp fire)

_____ **Musician** (to play a fiddle or harmonica in the evenings)

_____ **Animal guardian** (to feed and look after the horses, oxen, cattle, sheep and other animals)

_____ **Sharpshooter** (to hunt deer, rabbits, and other game)

_____ **Carpenter** (to make tools, utensils and to build caskets for those who die along the way)

_____ **Knitter/quilter** (to make blankets, coats, hats, gloves, etc)

_____ **Judge** (to resolve conflicts)

_____ **Sheriff** (to maintain law and order)

_____ **Interpreter** (to communicate with the Indians)

I Thought it was Your Dog!

Once upon a time a man whose ax was missing suspected his neighbor's son.

The boy walked like a thief, looked like a thief, and spoke like a thief.

But the man found his ax while digging in the valley, and the next time he saw his neighbor's son, the boy walked, looked, and spoke like any other child.

— Lao-tzu

Have you ever acted like this man? Have you ever accused or blamed someone, only to find out later you were wrong?

Have you ever been too quick to judge others? Have you thought things like, "He's so tall he must be a good basketball player," or "She's a girl, I can run faster than her," or "His name is Poindexter. He must be a nerd," or "She is very poor. She must have stolen the money." Has there ever been a time when you met someone for the first time and you didn't think you would like him, and then later the two of you become great friends?

Once there was a man named Ron who was invited to visit Henry's house for lunch. Henry and Ron worked at the same factory, and they wanted to talk business while having their meal. Henry gave Ron directions to his house.

When Ron arrived at the house, he noticed in the front yard, a very large dog, probably a Great Dane. He knocked on the door. Henry said, "Welcome! Come on in." As Ron entered, the huge dog brushed between their legs and ran into the house.

The two men ate lunch in the living room. While they talked, the dog was running all over the house. It jumped on furniture, chewed up a pillow, went to the bathroom on the floor, knocked over two lamps, pulled down some curtains, and chased the cat under the sofa. The house was a mess!

After an hour or so, Ron said, "Thank you for lunch, I need to return home." As they headed towards the front door, Henry asked, "Ron, do you always travel with your dog?" Ron said, "That's not my dog, I thought it was yours!" Henry replied, "No, that's not my dog, I thought it came with you."

Now, let's take a closer look at this humorous story. Although the dog was destroying the house, neither man said anything or tried to put the dog out. Henry thought the dog belonged to Ron, and Ron thought the dog was Henry's. During the visit, the men were probably saying these things to themselves:

Ron was thinking…"I can't believe that Henry lets his dog run around in his house. This dog is too big to be inside, and it's doing a lot of damage. His wife will be upset when she gets home."

Henry was thinking…"I can't believe this! Ron comes to visit and he lets his dog in the house without even asking. It is breaking and tearing up things, and bothering my cat, and he doesn't say or do anything about it. What a rude, uncaring person he is!"

So be careful not to be too quick to judge, blame, or accuse others. Just because Mary has chocolate on her face doesn't necessarily mean she stole your candy bar.

**Don't be too quick to jump to conclusions.
Make sure you know the "whole" story.**

ACTIVITY 21:
Jumping to Conclusions

Directions: Read the following short story then gather in a small group and discuss responses to the questions.

Chad has a younger sister who often goes into his room to borrow things. Quite often she forgets to return them. Chad can't find his calculator that he needs to do his math. He gets angry and rushes to his sister's room and yells at her, "Where's my calculator!" She gets upset and tells him that she doesn't have it. Chad continues to yell at her. Mom enters the scene and says, "Chad, stop yelling at your sister and clean up your room." As he straightens up his room he looks under his bed and sees his calculator!

1. Did Chad jump to a conclusion? ❑ YES ❑ NO
2. Why did Chad accuse his sister of taking the calculator? ______________________

   ____
3. Do you have a brother or sister who takes things from your room? ❑ YES ❑ NO
4. Have you ever been guilty of taking things from your siblings' rooms? ❑ YES ❑ NO
5. Does Chad owe his sister an apology? ❑ YES ❑ NO
6. Can you think of a time you jumped to a conclusion? How did you resolve the situation? Did you have to make an apology?

   ____

   ____
7. Can you think of a time someone accused you of something you didn't do? Were you wrongly punished? How did you feel? Did you receive an apology?

   ____

   ____

Monty's Essay: F or A+

Monty Roberts did not grow up in a wealthy family. During his childhood years, he worked with his father training horses. Together they traveled from town to town, and ranch to ranch, and many times had to sleep in barns and stables. Because of his travels, he attended several different schools, and at times, had to have a tutor travel with him to help keep up with his schoolwork.

As Monty traveled with his father, he always dreamed of having his own ranch. He wanted a 200 acre farm with a beautiful house, several race horses, and plenty of workers to keep the ranch running. He would often draw pictures and diagrams of his future ranch.

During his senior year in high school, one of his teachers gave the class a homework assignment. Monty and his classmates were to write an essay entitled, "My Goals in Life." The teacher reminded the class to be honest, but be realistic about their future plans. "I don't want to know about any Hollywood dreams either," noted the teacher. He added, "It should be a fair and accurate assessment of where I might find you if I were to visit you in your mid-thirties."

Monty was very excited about writing the essay. Of course, his seven page report went into great detail about his future 200-acre ranch, beautiful house, and race horses. He proudly turned in the paper to his teacher, and believed he was going to receive an A.

Several days later, he got his essay back. On the top of the first page was a large, red F with a note from the teacher saying, "See me." The teacher told Monty that he got the failing grade because his future goals were too unrealistic and too unbelievable. He lectured to Monty that it would be impossible to have such a huge home and ranch. He added, "It's a wild, unattainable dream. I gave you the F based on the instructions I issued — be realistic! I know your family and background, and you'll never have enough money to achieve your goal." The teacher told Monty that if he rewrote the essay he would consider giving him a higher grade.

Monty was very upset as he told his mother what had happened. He asked her advice. She encouraged him not to change the story. "If that really is your goal in life, then go for it," she said. The next day he told the teacher he would take the F, he wasn't going to write a different essay. Monty kept the paper with an F on the front of it and placed it in a glass frame, hung it on a wall, and looked at it every day as a motivator.

Over the years, Monty worked hard and finally got his ranch. He owned a 4,000 square foot home, 200 acres, many horses, and had several employees. School children

would often arrive in yellow buses to tour the ranch and have picnics on the grounds. One day, he received a phone call from a man who wanted to bring a bus load of visitors to see his ranch. The man's voice and name sounded familiar. Monty agreed to let his group visit.

When the bus arrived, Monty met it at the entrance to his ranch. What happened next was almost unbelievable. The leader of this tour group was the teacher who gave him the F on his essay back in high school many years ago! Imagine what that teacher must have been thinking when he realized it was Monty who owned the now-famous horse ranch!

Monty's former teacher admitted he had made a mistake by giving Monty a failing grade on the essay. He told the tour group about Monty and the essay. Monty never forgot what his teacher said to him and the people on the bus. "There was a time when I told Monty that this was unattainable. Now we've all had a look around and can see that he proved me wrong. A teacher does not have the right to put a cap on the aspirations of his students, no matter how unreal those aspirations might seem."

Set goals and go for them. Don't listen to others who tell you that you can't reach your goals.

ACTIVITY 22:
Career Goals

Directions: As a youngster Monty dreamed of operating his own horse ranch. Even though one of his teachers said he couldn't do it, he did! What career goals do you have? Do you often think about a certain type of job you would like to have when you're 25 or 30 years-old? Some jobs pay a lot but are very dangerous or stressful. Other jobs can be more enjoyable, less stressful but, may not pay well. Earning a decent salary is important but most adults will tell you there are more important aspects to a job than money.

According to a recent Job Related Almanac these are the ten most stressful jobs in the US. Next to each occupation, write a few words about why such a job would be so stressful. Most of these jobs pay well but they are not easy.

1. President of the US

2. Firefighter

3. Corporate Executive

4. Race Car Driver

5. Taxi Driver

6. Surgeon

7. Astronaut

8. Police Officer

9. NFL Football Player

10. Air Traffic Controller

The Eagles vs. the Chickens

William Avery was hiking through the woods on a cool spring morning. Along the way, he found a wounded baby eagle lying on the ground. One of the bird's wings was broken and it couldn't fly. He carried the bird back to his farm and he placed it in a box. William's goal was to help the eagle regain its strength so it would be able to return to the wild.

It took longer than he thought it would to repair the broken wing, so he decided to place the baby eagle in the yard with his chickens. This would allow it to move around and be near other creatures. Every morning William would sit, drink his coffee, and watch the eagle and the chickens. After a week or so, he began to notice some strange happenings. The eagle was beginning to act like the chickens. It would go in the chicken coop at dusk, and then leave the coop in the morning with the chickens. It spent most of the day walking around scratching the ground and pecking at insects, grain, and chicken feed.

Although William found this to be very interesting and comical, he realized that it was time to release the bird. It was healthy now and appeared ready to fly. One morning, he picked the eagle up and placed it on his arm. He told the eagle, "Go, fly away. You are an eagle, not a chicken. You are free to go. You are a protected bird that can soar in the sky, eat whenever you wish, and you represent freedom and glory, and our country." Again, William shouted at the bird to go, but all the eagle did was look at all the chickens on the ground in front of him. The eagle jumped back down on the ground, and again, acted like a chicken.

The next day, William placed the eagle on top of the chicken coop. Again he told the eagle, "Go, fly away. You are an eagle, not a chicken. Leave and be free. No one is allowed to kill you, and you can go wherever you want. You don't need to be hanging around a farm with chickens." All the eagle could see were the other chickens on the ground. He jumped off the coop and landed next to the chickens, and started pecking at the ground.

William had one final plan. He put the bird back in the box and traveled fifty miles in his truck. He climbed to the top of a tall mountain and placed the eagle on his arm. He again encouraged the eagle to fly, and he reminded the bird about his glory, freedom to fly anywhere, and his ability to see for miles, and eat whenever it wished. This time the eagle could not see his chicken friends. He looked around and flew away. Once in the sky, the eagle began to find out it is much better to be an eagle than a chicken. It soared alone high in the mountains. It enjoyed the beautiful scenery, and was even able to see a small mouse crawling in the grass from two

miles in the sky. It was a great feeling. The eagle lived a long healthy life in the mountains. He was an eagle, not a chicken.

This story has a powerful message. When the eagle hung around chickens, it started acting like a chicken. If you hang around the wrong type of people, will you begin to act like them? If you hang around other young people who steal, lie, smoke, cheat, or don't try to do well in school, will you begin to steal, lie, smoke, cheat and not do well? If you hang around young people who are honest, work hard, are involved in church and sports, and are successful students, you will begin to do the same things? Hundreds of years ago, there was a quote which said, "Tell me who you walk with and I'll tell you what you are."

Be an eagle, not a chicken. Chickens have no goals in life. Every day is the same. They get up early, peck and scratch in the yard, and go to bed at dusk. Eagles soar to great heights, appreciate freedom, and are respected by all.

Be careful in selecting your friends. They can influence you in a good way or a bad way.

ACTIVITY 23: Best Friends, Cliques, Crowds

Directions: By late elementary school and into middle school you become more influenced by your friends or peers. When you are with your peers you may actually do things that you know your parents do not want you to do. This is called peer pressure. Because of the crowd you are in, you may act a certain way to fit in or to be a member.

Laurence Steinberg, a nationally recognized expert in psychology, believes that an adolescent's social world can be drawn as three circles; best friends, clique, and crowd.

Best Friends: These are the friends that you feel closest to and with whom you spend most of your time. You talk to them often on the phone, eat lunch with them, walk with them in-between periods at school, and they may visit you often at home. Best friends compromise the inner part of the circle.

Cliques: The next circle out are fellow students who are considered friends but, not "best friends." These relationships may change from week to week. These clique members have similar interests. At any one time your clique will have six to ten members.

Crowd: The third circle is composed of other students who share certain features with you. You are a member of a certain crowd by virtue of your common interests, attitudes, and preferred activities. It is possible to be a member of a certain crowd without really knowing each other well at all. Students label crowds by such names as: jocks, populars, preppies, normals, nerds, brains, druggies, skate-boarders, freaks, stoners, burnouts, greasers, loners, red-necks, and partyers.

HERE ARE A FEW THINGS TO THINK ABOUT...

1. Who would you list as your best friends?

---

2. Can you think of at least six members of your clique?

---

3. Steinberg's research found that most teenagers say that they, themselves are unclassifiable but most teens have little difficulty in identifying which crowd their classmates belong to. In which crowd do you and your closest friends belong?

---

4. Are you and your best friends guilty of labeling other students? For instance, have you ever said something like this..."Sally is a 'preppie'"? ❑ YES ❑ NO

5. Do you believe it is OK to label others? ❑ YES ❑ NO

6. Are you pleased with the crowd you are in? Is your crowd helping or hurting you academically and behaviorally? ❑ YES ❑ NO

Can Marshmallows Predict Your Future?

"Patience is a virtue." Maybe you have heard your parents or teachers make this comment. What they are trying to tell you, is that having the abilities to stay calm, wait, and control your behavior, are very important life skills. Are you able to be patient, study hard, go to school for thirteen years, and if you want to, go another four years to college before getting or buying all those items you dream of? Are you able to control your emotions when the class bully hits you, or is your solution to hit back? Are you able to control your actions, and maybe think of a creative way to deal with the bully? Are you patient and willing to practice, practice, practice — in order to master a skill, or do you quit easily? Are you able to work part-time and save money for the special toy, CD or bicycle, or do you bug your parents — constantly asking for those items now?

Psychologists and educators have found that young people, who can master the skills of being patient, and the ability to control impulses, are usually more successful later on in life. One famous study by Psychologist Walter Mischel at Stanford University used marshmallows to prove the point. He tried an unusual experiment with four-year- olds, and then met with these same youngsters when they were in high school and then twenty years later when they were adults in their 30' and 40's.

Four-year-olds were placed in a small waiting room with hidden cameras. Each child sat at a desk, and a tasty, puffy marshmallow was placed in front of them. The adult told each child that they could eat the marshmallow now, or if they could wait for the adult to leave the room and run a short errand, when he returned — then they could have two marshmallows. This was a difficult problem for a four-year-old. "Should I eat the one marshmallow now, or can I wait a few minutes, and then I'll get two marshmallows?" Depending on which decision they chose as a four-year-old determines a lot about how successful they are in school — and life in general — when they are seniors.

The children who were able to sit and wait for the adult to return so they could get a second treat, were already developing skills to control their impulses. As witnessed on hidden camera, when the adult left the room, the children tried various strategies to keep them from grabbing the marshmallow. Some closed their eyes, talked to themselves, played games with their fingers, or even tried to sleep. They were able to wait for the adult to return and earned a second marshmallow.

When these same children were tracked down twelve to fourteen years later, the researchers found that they were doing well in school. Most of them got along well with others, were better able to cope with stress and frustration, were more confident, less apt to use drugs and/or alcohol, had less problems with authority figures, and scored quite high on the SAT (Scholastic Aptitude Test) used for college admissions. These children, when tracked down even later in life, were also found to be successful in their careers and marriages, and less likely to be involved with drugs or alcohol abuse.

The four-year-olds who could not wait for the adult to return and who ate the first marshmallow were found to have many more problems later in school and later as adults. These youngsters had not developed skills to be patient; they wanted the treat now! When this group was tracked down many years later, it was found that most of them were easily upset, more stubborn, got jealous often, overreacted to little problems, quick-tempered, more apt to use drugs, and get into trouble with the law. Most surprising of all, they scored much lower on the SAT than did the group of students who were able to control impulses and wait for a second marshmallow!

Learning to be patient, control impulses, and delay gratification are crucial life skills. Practice taking deep breaths or counting to ten when you get upset. Learn to avoid situations and other students who may place you in positions where it is difficult to "control" yourself. If necessary, seek help from trained adults.

Patience is a virtue. Slow down and control your impulses.

ACTIVITY 24: Stop...Caution...Go

"Why most people don't succeed is that they forgo what they want most for what they want at the moment."

I don't know who wrote this quote but, it makes a lot of sense. So many people are impulsive. They want things now instead of waiting for better things later. For instance, sixteen year-old Jamie knows she should stay home and study for finals because she needs to pass tenth grade. A couple of her friends encourage her to sneak out of town for the weekend for a wild party at the beach. She gives in and goes for the fun weekend even though she knows it may cause her to fail and delay her graduation for a year. Larry, captain of the football team, has a chance to earn a full scholarship to college. His friends kept "bugging" him about going out drinking. He gives in to their pleas. He gets drunk and kicked off the team…no scholarship!

If you are a person who has a problem controlling your impulses, try using the technique below.

Think of a traffic light, red, yellow, and green. When you start to get angry, over-react to something petty or small, or start to do something impulsive; think…

RED: Step back, cool down, take a deep breath, count to 10, etc.

YELLOW: Take two or three minutes to think about your choices. Should I or shouldn't I? What's the worst that could happen? Is it worth the risk? Is this going to help or hurt me reach my ultimate goals in life?

GREEN: Come up with a decision, talk your problem over with someone else, compromise, and devise a plan.

SUGGESTIONS:

1. Place a red, yellow, and green sticker on your desk. When you start to get impulsive look at the stickers. Touch the red one while you are "cooling" down, the yellow one while you think of your options, the green one as you follow through with the plan.

2. I know one girl who has a key chain shaped like a traffic light with the three colors. She looks at her key chain when she gets impulsive.

3. Draw a picture or get a poster with a traffic light on it. Put it on the wall in your room. When you encounter a difficult situation, go to your room and focus on your poster.

Where's My Little Girl

Martin and Jill lived in Los Angeles with their baby girl, Jodie. After a year in the big city, they decided to move their small family to a remote area of Alaska, away from crime, busy streets, and pollution, They wanted to raise their little girl where the air was clean, and where they would be able to appreciate nature.

Martin built a log cabin on a small hill that was located over fifty miles from their nearest neighbor. Jill would stay with Jodie, while Martin and his dog would go hunting, fishing, cutting trees, and trapping. The weather was often too cold to have Jodie tag along. They enjoyed their quiet, self-sufficient lifestyle — free from television, shopping malls, grocery stores, and noisy streets.

One day, Jill became very ill and because she was so far from a doctor or hospital, she died before help arrived. Martin was saddened and confused. What should he do? Should he return to the big city? How could he and Jodie survive in the wilderness without Jill? For several days he thought about his options. He decided to stay in Alaska with Jodie.

Since Jodie was so young, and the wilderness was so dangerous, Martin decided to train his trusty dog to stay in the cabin with her while he went out on his daily travels for food and wood. His dog would keep Jodie safe and warm.

Normally, Martin would only be gone for a few hours at a time. He was nervous leaving Jodie and the dog alone. One afternoon while out chopping trees, he was caught in a nasty blizzard. The snow was so heavy that he couldn't see but a few feet ahead of him. He decided to find shelter instead of risking the chance of getting lost. He was able to escape the blizzard's cold wind by hiding in a large hollow part of a tree trunk. He had to spend the night in this tight space. All night long he thought about Jodie. He had never left her alone this long. Would she be warm enough? Would his dog do his job and keep her safe?

The next morning the storm ended. Martin rushed home through the thick snow as fast as he could. When he got to his cabin, he noticed the front door was open. There was blood in the snow. As he started to enter the cabin, his dog met him at the door. The dog had blood on his fur and around his mouth and teeth. Martin thought the worst. "Oh no! My dog has killed my little girl!" He became wild with anger. He picked up his axe and struck the dog, killing it.

His anger finally leaves him as he sat on the steps of his cabin and began to cry. He lost his wife, his daughter, and his dog. He is all alone. He thinks about killing himself, when suddenly he hears a noise inside. He goes back inside, looks under his bed and sees Jodie.

She is alive, but she is scared and cold! He picks her up and hugs her. Thank God she's OK! As he holds her, he sees something next to his bed. It was a dead wolf that was obviously killed by his dog. Now he realizes that his dog had done its job. It killed a wolf that had entered the cabin. Martin had killed the dog that saved his girl's life!

Instead of controlling his anger, Martin's anger controlled him. If he had been able to "cool down" and think before he acted, he would have found his daughter alive, and he wouldn't have killed his dog.

It is crucial that you think before you act. When something happens that you don't like, step back, take a deep breath, and think before acting. If you can do that, you are less likely to do something that you will regret later. There is a Chinese proverb that says, ***"If you are patient in one moment of anger, you will escape a hundred days of sorrow."***

ACTIVITY 25:
My Boiling Point

Directions: Quite often you'll hear someone who is getting angry mention their "boiling point." Water boils at 212 degrees. Following are a dozen scenarios. After each one rate your degree of anger based on the 212 degree-scale with that number (212) being the highest down to zero degrees which means it doesn't anger you in the least.

_____ Another student crowds ahead of you on the way to lunch.

_____ Someone has spread a very hurtful lie about you on FACEBOOK.

_____ Aaron keeps forgetting to return the five dollars he borrowed from you.

_____ Your teacher accuses you of cheating.

_____ Your neighbor has a dog that is tethered twenty-four hours a day. It is never allowed off the chain.

_____ You missed making the Honor Roll by one point.

_____ One of your classmates made an unkind racial comment about your best friend.

_____ You didn't make the volleyball team but Sally, the mayor's daughter did, and you know you are much better than she is at playing volleyball.

_____ Kids are making fun of Hector's stuttering.

_____ You saw Juanita cheat on the test and didn't get caught.

_____ The teacher made the whole class have silent lunch even though you did nothing wrong.

_____ You see someone in the car ahead of you throw a bunch of trash along the road.

The 12-Year- Old King

Long ago, there was a very kind and wealthy king who lived in England. He had a beautiful castle and his kingdom covered many miles. He owned many sheep, had a cellar filled with gold, and numerous fruit fields. The king knew he was getting old and he would soon die, but since both of his sons died in battles, he had no one to inherit his valuable kingdom. Who should he give his belongings to? Whom could he trust to take over and be kind to the villagers? Will the new king be fair? Would the new leader be greedy and not share his wealth?

Who should he select? Every day he sat in the tower and pondered this question. When the word got out that the king was looking for a new leader, visitors began knocking on his door. Many men tried to convince the king that they were capable of taking over, but the king did not trust most of them. He believed they just wanted his kingdom in order to steal his money. Many requests were denied.

Whenever he sat in his tower, the king always noticed his young shepherd, John-Paul, hard at work. John-Paul was only 12-years-old, but the king was amazed at how well he did his job. The boy always arrived at work at dawn, never missed a day, never left the sheep unattended, fed them all on time, and he was not always asking for money or favors like so many other workers did. The king thought to himself, "John-Paul has all the qualities to be the new king, but he is so young — and how do I know if I can trust him?

More days went by, and more visitors begged the king to let them succeed him, but the king still did not feel any of them could be trusted. He knew he would die any day now. He had to do something soon. Again and again, his thoughts returned to John-Paul. The king finally decided to "test" John-Paul to see if he could be trusted.

One morning, the king dressed up in a disguise. He put on a big hat, fake beard, and raggedy old clothes. He looked like a beggar-man. The king in his disguise approached John-Paul and said, "I'm a stranger here and I am lost. I am almost blind and I need you to take me to the village of Cedar Falls. Please take me." John-Paul replied, "I will tell you how to get there, but I cannot leave the sheep." The old man again asked the young boy to take him. John-Paul said, "No, I have to stay with the sheep so wolves and thieves do not get them. That is the king's order. He has trusted me with his animals."

The stranger asked John-Paul several more times. He even offered the shepherd boy several bags of gold coins if he left the sheep to take him to town. No matter what was offered, John-Paul refused to leave the sheep. The king now knew he could trust the boy. He took off the hat and fake beard, and said to John-Paul, "Congratulations, you are now the new king."

It was trust and honesty that earned this poor shepherd boy his own kingdom at the age of twelve. Can you be trusted? Are you always honest and tell the truth?

To be trusted is one of the greatest honors in life.

ACTIVITY 26:
Who Do You Trust?

Directions: Think of at least three people that you feel you can trust. These people could be friends or adults. Also think of reasons why you trust them.

All through life we are put in a position where we need to trust others. We should trust our doctors, teachers, police, and our parents. We also want others to trust us just like the king trusted John-Paul, the shepherd.

Throughout history there were many times when people had to trust their leaders, explorers, scientists, and inventors. For instance, Christopher Columbus set out to prove that the world was round. He needed to have his ship's crew trust him because back then most people believed the world was flat. As he sailed and sailed for many days, some of his crew stuck with him. They had faith and trusted him while some men had doubts and considered turning back to Europe.

Person	**Why do you think you can trust him/her?**
____________________	______________________________
	______________________________
	______________________________
____________________	______________________________
	______________________________
	______________________________
____________________	______________________________
	______________________________
	______________________________

The Million Dollar Bathroom Break

Have you ever been travelling in a car when the sudden urge to go to the bathroom hits you? Did you cross your legs, grit your teeth, whistle a tune, and beg the driver to find a restroom as soon as possible? Holding it in can be painful. On practically every family vacation parents hear kids in the backseat yelling, "I can't wait. I got to go pee!" Then the parents ask, "Can you wait until we get to the amusement park?" The kids usually reply, "No. I'm going to wet my pants!" Now the pressure is on the parent who is driving the car. He or she needs to find a restaurant, service station or rest area as soon as possible.

Well, having to urinate during travels happens to adults as well as children. Let me tell you about one gentleman who suffered greatly trying to find a bathroom, then the unbelievable event that followed. He went from pain (holding it in) to pleasure (a celebration) in a matter of weeks. George was an insurance salesman who lived in Florida. One day while heading home he got lost in rural Georgia. He had been drinking a lot of coffee that morning and had to urinate. That uncomfortable feeling was getting worse; he had to go now! On the dusty back roads he couldn't find a restaurant or gas station. He couldn't deal with the pain anymore and made a decision to stop at the next intersection and visit the first building he came to. As he pulled off the main road the first building he spotted was a funeral home with one car in the parking lot.

George was unaware that a funeral was in the process. The funeral was for the small town's miser, Mr. Hanson who died a couple days ago. Mr. Hanson was a recluse. He had no friends or family. He was very rude and couldn't get along with anyone. No one in town realized that he had over a million dollars hidden in his small, dirty apartment. A few days before he died his lawyer asked him what should be done with the million dollars when he died. Since he didn't have any relatives or family he told the lawyer to divide his money up among all who attend his funeral. He said, "Anyone who comes to my funeral must care about me a little, so let them have the money." The lawyer agreed and said he would have a sign-in sheet with names and addresses of those who attend the funeral. Then he could mail the attendees their share of the money.

George rushed through the funeral home's open door and saw a man there (Mr. Hanson's lawyer) and he saw a dead man in a casket (Mr. Hanson), nobody else was there. George said to the lawyer, "I need to use the bathroom badly. Where is it? Can I use it?" George was squeezing his legs together and hopping around waiting for directions to the bathroom. The lawyer replied, "Before you use the bathroom you must sign in with your name, address, and telephone number." George replied, "I can't do that now, I've got to go pee!" Again the lawyer said told him to sign in first. George had no choice. He gritted his teeth while he signed the guest list. Then he bolted to the bathroom! On his way out he thanked the man for letting him use the facility.

Finally at 4:00 pm the funeral was over and the lawyer locked the front door. Then he looked over the sign-in sheet. Only one person, George, showed up for Mr. Hanson's funeral. A couple weeks later George answered his telephone at his Florida office. A man asked, "Are you George Hollister and did you sign-in at a funeral home last month?" George thought a minute then remembered his funeral home 'pit stop.' George replied, "Yes I did." The caller added, "Well, George, I'm Mr. Hanson's lawyer and he told me to divide up his savings among all who attended his funeral. You were the only one to show up. I'll be mailing you a check for approximately a million dollars. Have a nice day."

Being embarrassed is part of life; it happens to everyone.

ACTIVITY 27:
Oh, How Embarrassing!

Directions: All of us have suffered some embarrassing moments and here are a few examples. Read each one then decide how embarrassing it would be for you. Score each one on a 0-5 scale. Zero means it wouldn't bother you at all and a 5 would mean it would be extremely embarrassing to you. Remember; score each one with a 0, 1, 2, 3, 4, or 5.

_____ You walk up the hall with toilet paper stuck to your shoe.

_____ Another student, in front of others, says, "You've got bad breath!"

_____ You accidently burp in the cafeteria.

_____ You drop your tray of lunch on the floor in the cafeteria.

_____ You 'loudly' pass gas in class.

_____ When you bend over in gym class, your shorts rip.

_____ When the two captains select their softball teams, you are picked last.

_____ You are caught picking your nose in math class.

_____ In front of a large audience you forget the lines to your speaking part.

_____ In class the teacher tells the whole class that you got the lowest grade.

_____ At the end of the school day a student tells you that your two sock colors don't match.

_____ In the kickball game you try to kick the ball and miss and fall down.

I Wish...

Have you ever noticed how often people use the words, "I wish...?" You probably use those words more than you realize. There is nothing wrong with wishing for things, as long as you are honest and realistic. In fact, making a wish is actually the first step in setting a goal and if you work hard, you have a good chance of having your wish come true. But if you are the type of person who is always wishing for things and doesn't "act" on those wishes, then they probably will not come true. For instance, I can sit at my desk and say to myself, "I wish I had more money." But if I just sit there and not do anything, make excuses, and blame others — then my wish of having more money will not happen. I need to take action.

There are some important things you need to know about wishes. I've divided them into three categories. There are the 100%, 50% and 0% wishes.

100% Wishes: These are the wishes you make that you have control over. They are the ones that can come true no matter how rich or poor you are, if you have great supportive parents or parents who are not around, no matter your race, your gender, or what school you go to. Examples could be: wishing to do better on your next report card, becoming a good mechanic with your own shop when you get older, going to college, or learning how to play a musical instrument. All of these wishes can come true if you really work at them.

50% Wishes: These are the wishes that you do not have total control over, but you still have about a 50% chance of making them happen. For example: your bedtime may be 9:00, but there is a special show on TV tonight that you wish to see. If you have your chores and homework completed, and you ask your parents if you can stay up an hour later than normal, they may say yes. You may want to go see a new movie at the mall and if you politely ask your parents, you might actually go. Do not be afraid to share your wishes with others. If you don't, then others won't be able to help you get what you want. If there is a certain gift you would like at Christmas, then tell others. This will increase your chances of getting it.

0% Wishes: These are the wishes that you have no control over and because of that, they do not come true. No matter how hard you pray or wish, they cannot happen. For instance, if you're sitting in the principal's office and you say to yourself, "I wish I hadn't hit Jimmy in class." It's too late — you cannot change that. If your mother grounds you for two weeks and you say to her, "You're not fair. I wish I had a different mother." That desire will not come true. She will always be your mother. You may be 15-years-old and five foot tall. While playing basketball, you wish that you could be seven and a half feet tall so you can play center in the NBA. It won't happen.

Let's take a closer look at the 0% wishes. After you realize that these wishes won't happen, then you need to make an effort to still go on and be successful. Don't let the impossible dreams make you quit or give up on the future. Ray Charles, Ronnie Milsap, and Stevie Wonder are all blind. I bet each one of them wished at some time in their lives that they were not blind. They knew their sight could not be restored, but they still went on to become famous singers and pianists. Each one has sold several million record albums, cassettes, and CD's.

Jim Abbott wished he was born with two hands, but he wasn't. In 1993 he pitched a no-hitter for the New York Yankees. Zoe Koplowitz wished she didn't have multiple sclerosis, but she does. In 1993, on crutches, she completed the New York City Marathon (26.2 miles) in 24 hours! They both had a strong desire to accomplish their goals but they had to work harder than most. Always remember this quote, "You don't get what you wish for, you get what you work for."

You don't get what you wish for; you get what you work for.

ACTIVITY 28:
Worldly Wishes

Most wishes that people make are for things they want for themselves. Seldom do people wish for others. For this activity I'm going to ask you to think of a "worldly wish" aimed at helping people of all races and from all nations to get along better with each other in the future. Before you make your wish, read the three following quotes/wishes made by some well respected individuals.

"When we come to appreciate and value other people, even those who are very different from us in race or culture, our lives can become richer and fuller."

— Fred Rogers, Host of Mr. Rogers Neighborhood

"We must all stress family rituals and be moral examples for our children. If we cut corners, they will too. If we lie, they will too. If we spend all our money on ourselves and tithe no portion of it for our colleges, churches, synagogues, and civic causes, they won't either. And if we snicker at racial and gender jokes, another generation will pass on the poison my generation has not had the courage to snuff out."

— Marian Wright Edelman, Children's Defense Fund

"There is a Law that man should love his neighbor as himself. In a few hundred years it should be as natural to mankind as breathing or the upright gait; but if he doesn't learn it he must perish."

— Alfred Adler

MY WISH FOR THE FUTURE: ____________________

____

____

____

____

____

The Missionaries and the Mambas

Have you ever played a joke on someone and it backfired? Did you accidentally hurt your brother or sister when attempting to surprise or scare them? Playing practical jokes can be fun, but if you are not careful, something could go wrong and there could be serious consequences. Check out what happens in this story in which a husband tries to trick his wife!

Alan and Sylvia had been married for a couple of years when they decided to do some missionary work for their church. They were assigned to a special mission in southern Africa. Before they left the United States, they did a lot of studying about the culture of the country they were going to visit. They were both nervous and excited about living for two years in a strange country.

During their first week in Africa, they spent time with a local resident who was trained to orient them to their new setting. This teacher, Akil, taught Alan and Sylvia all he could about life in southern Africa, including the wildlife. He gave them skills needed to survive in a jungle filled with dangerous animals and poisonous snakes.

One afternoon, Akil and Alan were traveling along a dirt road about a mile from their village. Akil spotted a Black Mamba, which is the largest poisonous snake in Africa. This snake is fast-moving, slender, can grow up to 14 feet long, and is the most-feared snake on the continent. Akil thought it was important that Alan get a close look at the Black Mamba, so he killed it. Alan was amazed at its size. Akil warned Alan to be careful, because Black Mambas often travel in pairs, so another snake may be close by. Alan wanted to take the dead snake home so Sylvia could see what the Black Mamba looked like in case she encountered one on her travels. The snake was so long and heavy, that they had to drag it along the ground all the way back to Alan's small house on the edge of town.

Before entering the house, Alan decided he wanted to play a trick on Sylvia. He went through the back window into their bedroom, and coiled the dead snake on the floor next to the bed. He left through the window, but failed to close it all the way. He and Akil returned to the front of the house and entered. They greeted Sylvia and shared some tea. When Alan thought the time was right, he requested that Sylvia go in the bedroom and get his favorite pillow. As she headed toward the bedroom, Alan and Akil looked at each other and smiled. They knew she would scream when she saw the snake on the floor!

Sylvia goes into the bedroom and closes the door. The men await her scream, but nothing happens. It remained quiet. What happened? Didn't she see the snake? Alan waits another minute or two before going in to see what happened.

He opens the door and is shocked by what he sees. His wife was lying dead on the bed, and there were two snakes on the floor…the dead one and its mate, which had followed the scent of the dead snake as it was dragged along the path. The second snake had entered through the partially opened window and bit Sylvia when she entered the room. Apparently, she was so frightened that she passed out before being bit. Akil was able to kill the second snake.

Alan never wanted to hurt his wife, only wanted to scare her. His practical joke had backfired. Be careful!

Be careful when playing tricks or jokes on others. They can backfire.

ACTIVITY 29:
Oh No, My Trick Backfired!

I remember as a young boy I liked to play jokes and tricks on my younger brother. One time I snuck up behind him and poked him in the "behind" with a sharp pencil. I was hoping he would jump and go "ouch!" I never intended to really hurt him. Of course he went running to Mom. When she investigated his "behind" she noticed that pieces of wood and lead from the pencil had broken off and were stuck in his skin. She couldn't remove the pieces with the tweezers so she had to rush him to the hospital. I was in big trouble!

Let's talk tricks!

What was the funniest trick ever played on you? ______________________

____

____

What was the funniest joke you ever played on someone?

____

____

Can you take a joke? Do you seek revenge?

____

____

Have you and/or your friends ever played a joke/trick on someone that backfired? Did anyone get hurt? Did you apologize?

____

____

A Hug or a Handshake?

***"We need 4 hugs a day for survival.
We need 8 hugs a day for maintenance.
We need 12 hugs a day for growth."***

— Virginia Satir

King Frederick II was a very unusual leader. Back in the thirteenth century, he conducted a rather strange experiment. He wanted to see what language children would speak if they never had the chance to hear the spoken word. Would they speak German, French, Spanish, or some other language? He assigned foster mothers to look after 50 babies. The ladies were told to clean and feed the babies, but they were never allowed to hold, fondle, or play with them, and of course, they couldn't talk to them.

King Frederick's experiment failed because all 50 babies died! Even though they were fed and cleaned, they never made it to their first birthday. Even centuries ago, people began to realize that babies and children need love, holding, fondling, rocking, and other forms of human touch to survive.

Another example of the importance of love, touch, and nurturing, happened in Germany after World War II. A British nutritionist was puzzled by her observation that children in two different orphanages were growing at an alarmingly different rate, even though they were fed exactly the same food. The first orphanage had a kind, loving, caring supervisor who hugged and played with her babies and children every day. Her youngsters gained weight quickly and appeared happy. The second orphanage had a mean, strict leader. She never showed any affection towards the children. Her children were not gaining weight fast enough, got sick often, and appeared sad.

Then a strange thing happened. The kind, passionate leader of the first orphanage had to leave her job. She was replaced by the strict, uncaring supervisor from the second orphanage. Once she took over, the children in the first orphanage started to suffer. Their weight dropped, and many of them became ill and unhappy. This example again proves that children need to be hugged and touched on a regular basis in order to be happy and healthy.

Everybody needs to be loved. Everybody needs hugs, handshakes, pats on the back, shoulder rubs, and a tickle now and then. Babies need to be rocked, squeezed, and sung to. People who receive a lot of human touch tend to get sick less often, are happier, better able to handle stress, get along better with others, more likely to trust others, and are more likely to stay away from drugs.

I know a teacher who greets his fourth graders every morning at the door. He starts their day with, "Good morning! What's your choice — a hug or a handshake?" This teacher realizes that a special touch in the morning will help each child feel loved and important, and each child may then be more successful with his or her schoolwork.

So…I encourage everybody to hug more often. Sometimes your parents may seem to be busy and have not hugged you lately. You don't have to wait — you take charge and hug them. Parents need hugs too. If you see your grandmother coming at you like a Chicago Bears linebacker, don't run away! Grandparents need hugs too. Don't forget to hug your pets also!

Human touch is critical in the development of happy, successful people; so hug a lot!

ACTIVITY 30:

Hugs, Handshakes, Touches, & High Fives

Directions: We all have our own tolerance level when it comes to touching. Some of us love hugs from grandmothers while others may feel a bit uncomfortable. You might enjoy a back rub from your mother but not from an uncle you don't like. Many teens still kiss their parents and others might not think its "cool." What is an acceptable touch to one person may be unacceptable to another.

Take a few minutes to complete this exercise. It will help you determine which touches are acceptable to you. How comfortable would you be in the following situations? Answer each with "yes," "maybe," or "no."

	YES	NO	MAYBE
1. Your coach shakes your hand after the game.	❍	❍	❍
2. Your favorite grandparent greets you with a big hug.	❍	❍	❍
3. A new student pinches you on your bottom.	❍	❍	❍
4. A stranger pokes your arm to get your attention.	❍	❍	❍
5. The team captain gives you a "high five" after you score.	❍	❍	❍
6. Your best friend tickles you in the ribs.	❍	❍	❍
7. Your favorite aunt gives you a shoulder rub.	❍	❍	❍
8. Your favorite actor or actress gives you a hug.	❍	❍	❍
9. On your first date your partner tries to hold your hand.	❍	❍	❍
10. Your father kisses you "good night" on the cheek.	❍	❍	❍
11. You ask a stranger for directions. He puts his arm around you.	❍	❍	❍
12. While waiting in line for lunch, an older student pushes you.	❍	❍	❍

Should I or Shouldn't I?

Jermaine and his mother lived in a small, one bedroom apartment in one of the worst low-income housing projects in Baltimore. His neighborhood was a dangerous place. Drug dealers would meet on the playgrounds, and almost every night Jermaine could hear gunshots outside his window. No one dared to venture out after dark.

Jermaine's mother worked three different jobs, and was able to save a small amount to help him when he went to college. She refused to let him get a job. She wanted him to focus on his studies and sports. He reached his senior year in high school, and was an all-conference tight end on the football team. His mother's dream of him going off to college was nearing.

On a cold late October evening, he finished football practice and headed to the parking lot to wait for his uncle to pick him up. He waited for well over an hour and his ride did

not come. He didn't have money for a taxi, and he thought about walking the two miles to his apartment. Hundreds of times his mother warned him not to walk the streets alone at night, but it was getting late, he was cold, and he had a lot of homework to do. Against his mother's orders, he started towards home.

As he entered one of the most dangerous blocks in the area, he could hear a lady screaming for help just one street over. He continued to walk in the dark and tried to ignore this unknown lady's plea for help. He told himself, "I can't stop, I'm late and need to get home before mom does, so she doesn't find out that I walked home."

The screams got louder. He thought, "Should I help?" It would be risky and maybe he shouldn't get involved. The screaming got louder and he knew he had to do something to help. As he approached the scene, he could barely see two men hitting and kicking a lady. One of them had a knife. Fear left him as he charged them and yelled. The men ran off and he hovered over the lady. He couldn't see her face, but he could tell she was hurt. He said, "Lady, are you alright?" There was a pause, with several seconds of silence. Then the lady asked, "Jermaine, is that you?"

Yes, he took a risk and the lady's life he saved was his mother's. Sometimes in life you have to take risks. It is so easy to ignore and pretend you don't see anything or hear anything. Reach out and help others, a lady in need of help may not be your mother, but she is somebody's mother. However, if the situation involves a weapon, such as a gun or knife, go for help before putting yourself in danger.

Sometimes in life you have to take risks.

ACTIVITY 31: Risk Taking

Directions: Jermaine took a risk. He got involved and it was a good thing that he did. The person he saved was his mother! Throughout life everyone is placed in difficult situations where they don't really know what to do. Should I or shouldn't I get involved? Do I take a risk?

Here are some events that could happen to you. What would you do?

---

1. Joseph, the school bully, steals a book in the library. He knows that you saw him do it. He says, "If you rat on me, I'll get ya!"

---

2. One of your best friends shows you her back which is severely bruised from a beating from her father.

---

3. You get to school and realize you forgot to take your jackknife out of your pocket. This happens the day after the school principal tells the student body that she is calling the police if she finds another weapon at school. Do you 'risk' carrying it around?

---

4. At the corner store, Todd and Lillie steal candy bars. They dare you to steal one.

---

5. You are at a swimming pool and a little child falls in and starts to drown. You are not a good swimmer but there are no adults around.

---

6. You know three students who cheated on the last test. The teacher asks you if you saw anyone cheating.

---

7. At a party you see Jill, president of the school's SADD (Students Against Drunk Drivers) get drunk and starts to drive away in her mother's car.

Strength Coaching

Bob Bowman, a well-known workshop presenter, motivational speaker, and professor at the University of South Carolina, often mentions the term "strength coaching." He believes as I do, that everybody has a strength or something that they are good at. Your strength may not be math or science, but it could be art, sports, music, humor, or helping others. Dr. Bowman encourages young people to build on their personal strengths. For instance, if you are good at writing poems, then how can you use that talent to keep you busy, to help others, to prepare for a career in writing, or use your talent to help you in other areas of life?

Abebe Bikila's strength was his running. He was born in Ethiopia in 1927. Ethiopia was a very poor country. If you were born into a wealthy family, then you had a pretty easy life, but if you were born into poverty, like Abebe, then life was tough. Like so many of his countrymen, he lived in poor housing with no electricity, often went hungry for days, and lived miles from schools and shops. He had only a few pieces of clothing to wear, and did not own any type of footwear.

In order to get to school or town, Abebe would always run, and over the years he got to be quite good. No one in town could run faster, and he always ran barefoot. In 1960, he was sent to the Olympics in Rome, to run the marathon (26.2 miles) for his country.

When he lined up to start the race, runners from other nations stared and laughed at him because he was barefoot. They all had fancy running shoes and he was barefoot! They asked him how he was going to navigate all the hard streets and trails. He explained that he had always run without anything on his feet, so he wasn't going to change now.

Abebe went on to win the gold medal in that race. Four years later, he won the marathon again, this time at the Tokyo Olympics, and he broke the world's record. He became a hero in his country, for which the government actually rewarded him with a brand new Volkswagen car. It was quite an honor to own a vehicle in Ethiopia. In 1969, he was in a car accident that destroyed the nerves that directed his legs. Even though he was confined to a wheelchair, he went on to support and coach other young runners. He died in 1973.

Abebe used his exceptional skill of running to help him be successful in life. What is your strength? If yours is humor, instead of being the class clown, can you join the drama club, write the "funnies" for the school newspaper, or can you ask your teacher if you can visit other classes to tell funny stories? If you are good in art, can you draw pictures for the school newspaper, or assist the art teacher? If you are good at basketball, can you join the recreational department team, go to a basketball camp, or help younger students learn how to dribble and shoot?

Whatever your strength is, go for it! What you are good at today can be improved on, and it may lead you to a successful career. One final note here; everyone could benefit from having a coach. Find an adult that you respect to help you. He or she will be your support, cheerleader, and trainer. Hopefully, your parents can act as coaches, but if they can't, then ask a teacher, counselor, mentor, coach, relative, neighbor, or someone at church.

Everybody has a strength or something they do well. Take advantage of it!

ACTIVITY 32: What's Your Strength?

Directions: I believe that everyone has a strength; something that they do well. It could be running, humor, artistic ability, growing plants, playing a musical instrument, acting, or singing. I encourage young people to build on their strengths. Sometimes your special talents can lead to a successful career. Chris Rock's strength is humor. Mother Teresa's strength was helping others. Evander Holyfield's strength is boxing. What is yours?

Answer these questions. They may help you identify your special ability if you haven't found it yet.

1. What is your strength/special ability?

2. What are you doing presently to utilize your strength?

3. Can you name a famous person who has the same strength as you?

4. What type of career or jobs could you get with your special strength?

5. Presently, can you do some volunteer work to help others that could benefit from your special talent?

6. How will your strengths help you to get along better with others?

7. Below write a plan. Your plan should be for one year. It should include several strategies that will help you improve your strengths.

Who Is the Real Dummy?

Rarely does a student make it through elementary school without being teased. Some teasing is harmless, but quite often name-calling can be very hurtful. If a student informs me that he/she is being teased, I try to ease the pain by saying something like, "You don't have a problem, he (the person who is teasing) has the problem. His problem is that he is not being very nice."

I encourage students to ignore the teasing, but that does not always work. Other times I work with children to help them to be clever and creative when dealing with other not-so-nice peers. The following are two situations where the students who were being teased out-smarted their rude classmates.

Calvin and the Coins

Calvin was a quiet first-grader. Most of the time he played by himself and did not talk much. Other classmates did not bother him, except for Larry, the class bully. Whenever the teacher was not around, he would try to fool Calvin with his coin trick. Larry would take out a nickel and a dime. We know that although a dime is smaller, it is worth more money than the larger nickel. Larry believed that Calvin was not smart enough to know the difference.

Larry would put the two coins in his hand and walk up to Calvin. Larry would shout to the students, "Hey, watch this!" A small crowd would circle the two boys, and soon they would snicker as Larry began his daily trick.

"Here Calvin, you can have one of these coins," said Larry. Calvin, as usual, took the bigger coin — the nickel, and soon all the students would laugh and point at Calvin, calling him a dummy. This event happened almost every day. Calvin would take the nickel, and the students would tease him.

Finally, one day the teacher witnessed the event. After Calvin took his usual nickel, she asked him to come up to her desk. "Calvin," she said, "how long has this been going on, and why did you take the nickel instead of the dime? You know that a dime is worth more!"

Calvin responded, "Yes, I know a dime is worth more, but if I took the dime instead of the nickel, then he wouldn't do the trick on me again. I have a big jar of nickels at home. I'm saving the money to buy a toy." While everybody in class thought that Calvin was the dummy, he was actually the smart one. He kept letting Larry tease him, and he kept taking Larry's money! Soon, others in the class realized that Calvin was quite clever, and seldom was he teased after that.

Brittany's Books

Almost every day, two boys would hide Brittany's book bag. She would yell at them, tell the teacher, and some days, she would even cry. Nothing seemed to help. Something had to be done, because this was becoming very aggravating to her!

One day, she came up with an idea. She would use reverse psychology. She told the boys that she enjoyed having them hide her books, and she was now willing to pay them each a dollar a day if they would hide her books. For the next few days, she did pay them a dollar each. Then she told them that her allowance was cut, so she could only pay them 50¢ each a day. The boys still took her book bag and collected their 50¢.

A week later, she told the boys that her money was running low, and she could afford to pay them only 10¢ a day. The boys got angry and told her that they would no longer take her book bag if she was going to give only 10¢ a day! The boys stopped hiding her books. Her clever plan had worked!

ACTIVITY 33: Clever with Coins & Dollars

Directions: In our story we found out that Calvin was pretty clever when it came to coins and money. How clever are you? Try solving these by yourself or in a group. Check the back of the book for the answers.

1. What fifty coins have a total value of exactly one dollar?

2. Why are 1991 pennies worth almost twenty dollars?

3. Tommy's mother has three children represented by these three coins....a penny, a nickel, and a dime. The first child is named Penny. The second child is named Nichole. What is the name of the third child?

4. What very common item can be purchased at a hardware store and is priced similar to the schedule below?

   1 costs $ .50
   12 costs $1.00
   144 costs $1.50

Mr. Lincoln's and Henry's Shocking Experience

Henry will never forget the date — January 17, 1907. It was the first day at his new school. He and his dad had just moved to the Midwest from New York. It was an extremely cold day as he entered the small one-room schoolhouse for the first time. Even inside it was cold, so he kept his loose-fitting winter coat on. He walked up to the schoolmaster to introduce himself, but before he could get a word out, the stern, older man grumbled, "Oh, you must be the new kid. Just give me your first name, last name, and age, and then find a seat somewhere." The nervous boy responded, "Henry Thompson is my name and I am ten-years-old."

Henry squeezed in between two other boys. None of the students smiled or greeted him. The room was completely silent. Little did Henry know that his schoolmaster, Mr. Lincoln, just happened to be one of the cruelest teachers ever. He never smiled, praised, or talked to his students. He kept a thick stick on his desk and he used it daily to "discipline" the students. He never hesitated to smack a kid on the bottom, or rap their knuckles if they misbehaved, or if they gave the wrong answers to questions.

One of the worst things Mr. Lincoln did, was to focus on each students' weak points. Then he would humiliate them. In this year's class was a girl named Mary, who was very shy and stuttered a lot. Mr. Lincoln would make her stand in front of the class and read aloud. As she stumbled over the words, other students would laugh at her. He would make Larry, the smallest student, fetch several buckets of coal every day, and then he would make fun of him for being so weak. Then there was Ginger. She had a learning problem and always reversed her letters. Because of this, she could never get a 100 on a spelling test, and was punished by standing in the corner for hours at a time. It wouldn't be long before this schoolmaster found Henry's weakness.

At lunch time, Mr. Lincoln called Henry up to his desk to go over the long list of class rules. He shouted, "Young man, you are in my class now, so let me explain how we do things. I make the rules, and you obey them! When I call on you to recite, I want you to stand to the left side of your desk, say you name loudly, hold your textbook in your right hand, and then recite!" Henry tried to respond, "But sir, I can't hold the book in my right hand, I…" Mr. Lincoln would not let him finish and said, "Don't you question or back talk me, now sit down!" Henry returned to his seat.

Later that day, the schoolmaster called on Henry to recite. He stood to the left of his desk, said his name loudly, and held his textbook in his left hand. Mr. Lincoln was furious as he yelled, "I told you to hold your book in your right hand, not your left, you idiot!" Mr. Lincoln thought he had found Henry's weakness; he didn't know his left from his right.

Again, the schoolmaster yelled at Henry telling him to hold the book in his right hand. Every time Henry tried to say something, Mr. Lincoln would tell him to be quiet and, "Don't be disrespectful!" Thinking that the boy was defying him, Mr. Lincoln ran at the boy, shook him harshly, and pushed him down. As Henry fell to the floor, his jacket came off. Mr. Lincoln looked down, and was stunned to discover that Henry had no right arm, just a loose shirt sleeve dangling from his right side. Henry couldn't put the book in his right hand, because he did not have one! He tried to tell the teacher, but he wouldn't listen.

Everybody has a weakness or two. They might be afraid of heights, are sensitive about their weight, or are scared to speak in front of a group. We should do our best to not tease others about their weaknesses or sensitive issues. If you hated your freckles, or you were afraid to dive from a high board, would you want others making fun of you?

Don't tease others. We all have weaknesses.

ACTIVITY 34:
Sarcasm leads to "scarcasm."

Directions: Many years ago the education expert A. S. Neil said, "To be sarcastic to a child is to make the child feel inferior and degraded. Only a nasty teacher or parent will ever be sarcastic." When people are sarcastic to us, it can hurt and seldom do we forget their rudeness. Their negative words leave us with internal scars. I'm 62 years old but I still remember the day my eighth grade teacher said to me, "Tom, you haven't got enough sense to come in from the rain." I once counseled a fifty year-old woman who refused to chew gum because when she was a child her mother told her, "You chew like a cow chews its cud."

Sarcasm is often difficult to ignore or forget. Can you think of times an adult or classmates were sarcastic to you?

Three times that I remember someone being sarcastic to me.

1. What the person said to me ______________________

____

*How did it make you feel? ______________________

____

2. What the person said to me ______________________

____

*How did it make you feel? ______________________

____

3. What the person said to me ______________________

____

*How did it make you feel? ______________________

____

The Worst Feeling in the World

I believe one of the worst feelings in the world happens to thousands of students everyday in classrooms, and on the playground. It occurs when students are asked to "choose sides." Two students are selected to be leaders or captains, and they alternate back and forth choosing others for their team. Someone has to be the last one picked. Is there a worse feeling than being the last one chosen? I remember being one of the first ones picked for kickball in elementary school, but I also remember being one of the last chosen for spelling competitions. I felt terrible, nervous, and humiliated knowing that I wasn't wanted. If you are ever in a position to select others for your team — be fair. Give everyone a chance. Take a risk and choose a student that normally gets picked last. Years, weeks, and even days from now, you probably won't remember if your team won or lost. But by picking teammates that do not usually get picked early, you have accomplished much more than winning a game; you have helped others feel better and important.

The following is one of my favorite poems. It paints a good picture about how it feels to be chosen last.

Choosing Sides

By Angelyn Hall

Thick rimmed glasses
Masking tape across the nosepiece
Frail stature, skinny legs — portrait of a nine-year-old.

It was that time again — worst day of every week.
The day they'd play softball in Phys. Ed.
Feigning an illness — any illness,
Waking up early to drink hot coffee
To raise his temperature above the normal mark —
But his Mama knew the trick

So now he stood there,
Hands in his pockets, shuffling his feet,
waiting to hear his name.

Choosing teams and knowing he'd be last,
Not even his friends would want him.
Please, don't let him be last again.
Didn't they know he'd practiced,
How he could catch so much better now?

Yet he knew the outcome all too well — there'd be no one left but him.
Then they'd snicker and shake their heads Saying loudly — as if he weren't standing right there — "You take him."
"No, you. We don't want to lose."

They, ignorant of their own cruelty — or maybe not.
and he'd hang his head,
Knowing all his classmates had heard the public humiliation —
His silent walk to the gallows.

Who was the unfeeling human
Who's started the practice of choosing sides?
Oh destroyer of self-esteem.
Ten to one — he'd never been a little boy
Who'd stood there waiting for his name.

ACTIVITY 35:
Oh, That's Easy!

Directions: Here's something else that could cause you to feel terrible. The teacher passes out an exam or worksheet. You take a glance at it and realize how difficult it is; you don't know how to complete it and /or you think it is just too difficult. Then, across the room you hear another student say, "Oh, this is easy!" Has a teacher ever said this, "Everyone should know the answer to this question."? But, you didn't know the answer!

Try the following activity. Some of you will think it is easy while others my struggle.

In each of the sentences below, the name of an animal is concealed. The first sentence is marked so you can see how the word "dog" is hidden. Can you find the animal in each of the other sentences? Answers are in the back of the book.

Find the Hidden Animals

1. "What shall I do, Gertrude?" ______________________
2. Asking nutty questions can be most annoying. ______________________
3. A gold key is not a common key. ______________________
4. Horace tries in school to be a very good boy. ______________________
5. People who drive too fast are likely to be arrested. ______________________
6. "Did I ever tell you, Bill, I once found a dollar?" ______________________
7. John came late to his math class. ______________________
8. I enjoy listening to music at night. ______________________
9. The coin slot holds only quarters. ______________________
10. For lunch do you wish to have my tasty broth or Sela's soup? ______________________
11. Next Thursday we are going to Adventure Land. ______________________
12. Amos quit on Thursday. ______________________

Compassionate Passengers on the Slave Ships

Most of us have heard horror stories about the slave ships that transported millions of human beings from their homeland to America. The great African-American scholar-activist W. E. B. DuBois had this to say about this era. He called it, "The most significant drama in the last thousand years of human history—the transportation of ten million human beings out of the dark beauty of their mother continent into the new-found Eldorado of the West." More recent research uncovers the fact that during the almost four hundred years of the slave trade, 12.4 million souls were loaded onto slave ships and along the way 1.8 million died.

These captives were packed tightly on ships. They were beaten, starved, denied water, and suffered in the heat. Many died from the abuse and diseases and their bodies thrown overboard. Large groups of sharks often followed the slave ships and gobbled up the dead. But it wasn't just the black slaves that were tossed; many white crew members also became shark food. Let me explain.

As the slave ships were being loaded for their trips across the Atlantic, the captains had to round up a large number of crew members. The captains promised these men food, sleeping cabins, and a good salary that was to be paid at the end of the journey. The crew men had to follow the captain's orders on the trip or they would be severely punished. They worked long hours with meager food allotments. The crew was in charge of monitoring the slaves and was told to use whatever means necessary to keep the slaves in line. The more the crew members were mistreated, the angrier they got and often took out their frustrations on the helpless slaves. Many times these men complained that they were treated worse than the slaves.

Many captain's pay was based on the number of 'live' slaves they delivered. So they really wanted to prevent the loss of too many slaves, but if they lost a few crew members on the trip, it wouldn't affect their pay. Thousands of crew members were thrown to the sharks for being defiant, lazy, or for not being strict enough with the slaves. Remember, crew members were to be paid at the end of the journey, so whenever a captain hurled one of them overboard, it would be one less salary he had to pay. Also, there were many incidences of captains not paying their crew once they came ashore.

For the few crew members that did survive the journey, life was miserable. They roamed the docks. No one would hire them for fear of infection. They had no money

for food and slept under bridges. They were weak, skinny, bruised, and had bloody gums from scurvy. Many had the shakes and sweats of malaria. They were doomed! But guess who came to their rescue?

In his book, *The Slave Ship*, author Marcus Rediker writes, "An officer in the Royal Navy, a Mr. Thompson, noted that some of these pathetic sailors died but upon others the negroes have taken compassion and carried them into their huts." Rediker also tells how many of the former women slave ship passengers nursed the men back to health. They fed and clothed them and, through their own charity, buried the sailors when they died.

I bet many of you are thinking, "How could the slaves be so nice to the crew members who beat them, abused them, and treated them as non-humans?" Marcus Rediker helps us to better understand their actions. He writes, "What was the meaning of this compassion and charity? Is it possible that those who had survived the slave ship as prisoners knew precisely how horrible the experience had been for everyone aboard and that, moved by such knowledge; they could show sympathy and pity to those who had been their prison guards? Might the term 'shipmate' have been generous and bighearted enough to allow the oppressed to show humanity to the very people who had presided over their enslavement aboard the slave ship?'

Always practice the Golden Rule.

ACTIVITY 36: How Do You Show Compassion?

Directions: Answer the following questions.

What would you do?

You see a cold, hungry homeless person holding out an empty coin cup.

During a cold winter day you see birds scratching at your empty bird feeder.

You see an elderly man struggling to carry his bags of groceries.

You notice a new student doesn't have money to purchase pencils at the school store.

The person ahead of you in line at the burger stand needs 25 more cents to pay for his order and you have a pocket full of quarters.

Your church is having a canned food drive for the local food bank.

You see someone abusing a dog.

You notice that your elderly neighbor hasn't been out to get her newspaper for three days in a row.

Your mother is ill and the laundry needs to be done.

Several kids are making fun of the way Juan talks.

A Cow Hit Our Boat!

Randall lived in the United States for the first thirty years of his life. He earned a living catching and selling fish in Maine. He had always been interested in the Japanese culture and decided to take a major risk, and move his small company to the city of Sakata, which is located on the Sea of Japan.

During his first week there, he hired two young men, Masa and Kobo, to operate one of his fishing boats. From the start, both of these men caused nothing but trouble. Many days they wouldn't show up for work. They always lied and made up stories about being sick. Several times, Randall caught them drinking beer on the job. Randall even suspected them of stealing fish and equipment. Masa and Kobo could no longer be trusted. Randall decided to fire both of them.

Later on, the two young men returned and begged to be rehired. They promised to do a better job and be more honest. Randall, having mixed emotions, gave them another chance. He told them, "One more problem, and it's all over for good. I'll make sure you'll never be able to get a job anywhere in Sakata!"

On their first day back, Randall showed them his new $45,000 boat. Randall said, "Now take good care of this boat, and bring me back a ton of fish!" Early on a Saturday morning, Masa and Kobo left port and headed out to sea. They wanted to prove to their boss that they could once again be trusted, hard-working, and reliable employees.

By Sunday night, they had more than a ton of fish, so they headed towards home. They were about 300 miles from Sakata, when they heard a loud banging noise on the side of the boat. Masa told Kobo to check it out. Kobo returned and said, "Masa you are not going to believe this. There is a large cow trying to get in the boat!" Masa replied, "You are right. I don't believe you. We are 300 miles from shore. What would a cow be doing out here in the middle of the sea?" Masa went to see for himself, and sure enough, there was a dairy cow banging on the boat trying to get in! The cow left several dents and scratches on the side of the new boat. The cow's actions almost caused the boat to sink before Masa could steer it away.

Masa and Kobo knew they were in trouble. When their boss saw the damage to the boat, they would be fired, and they knew he wouldn't believe that the damage was done by a cow, hundreds of miles from shore. Masa and Kobo were right. Randall did not believe them, so he had them arrested.

Later that night, as Masa and Kobo sat in their jail cells, Randall sat down at his computer to get the latest local and world news. Imagine his surprise when the following news release came on the screen...

SPECIAL NEWS RELEASE: From the Russian Government TO: All Nations and People Living Near the Sea of Japan Date: May 12, 1998

Please be informed that on the evening of May 11, 1998, a Russian Agricultural Transport Aircraft was carrying a large cargo of supplies and farm animals over the Sea of Japan. During the flight, one large dairy cow got very nervous and became uncontrollable. In order to secure the safety of the other passengers and crew the cow was pushed from the plane over the Sea of Japan. We apologize for having to take such extreme action.

Masa and Kobo had indeed told the truth! Randall left his office and went to the jail to get them out.

Being honest and always telling the truth is so important. Others need to trust you. As in the case of Masa and Kobo, they lied so often that even when they were telling the truth, no one believed them. I am sure most of you know that if you do something wrong and get caught, you are in trouble with your parents/guardians. But, if you do something wrong and lie about it, then you are in double trouble!

ACTIVITY 37: True or False?

Directions: In the story Masa and Kobo had lied so often that even when they told the "true" event about a cow hitting their boat, their boss didn't believe them. How do you know when someone is not being honest with you? Has there ever been a time when you were telling the truth to a teacher and she didn't believe you?

Here are ten events. Are they true or false? Answer each with a "T" or "F."

______ 1. Henrietta Green (1835-1916) lived on cold oatmeal because she was too cheap (miserly) to heat it, in spite of the fact that she owned a fortune estimated at 95 million dollars.

______ 2. The women of southern India's Toda tribe are given two garments during their entire lifetime: one when they are children, the other when they are married.

______ 3. Ignatz von Roll, a turkey farmer from Germany, fitted all his turkeys with tiny Turkish turbans (hats), believing that if his birds wore the headgear, after awhile they would produce offspring of little turkeys with little hats on their heads.

______ 4. Anyone who said something funny to Tamerlane (1336-1405), the Mongol conqueror, was immediately put to death.

______ 5. Eugene Schneider of Carteret, New Jersey, was sued for divorce by his wife in July of 1976. The court ordered Eugene to divide his property equally between his wife and himself. He took the judgment literally, got out his chain saw, and cut the couple's home in two.

______ 6. According to Guinness, Chile's Atacaca Desert went 400 years without rain.

______ 7. King Cobra snakes kill an average of 10,000 people every year in India.

______ 8. On May 3, 1973, Robert Matern, set a record by eating 83 hambergers in two and a half hours.

______ 9. Zeuxis, a Greek painter in the 5th century B.C., laughed so hard at another artist's painting of an ugly old woman that he burst a blood vessel and died.

______ 10. During the entire run of NBC's "I Dream of Jeannie" (1965 – 1970), star Barbara Eden was never allowed to display her navel (belly button).

Rachel Never Told Her Dad

It was raining hard, and a strong wind was blowing in Rachel's face as she stood at the starting line. As she waited for the High School Conference Cross Country Championship Race to begin, many thoughts went through her head. She was a senior, so this would be her last chance to win a conference title. Standing next to her was Cynthia "Flash" Fergusen, from Mountain View High School. Was this going to be the year that she finally beat the "Flash?" Rachel wanted so badly to win the race. She had been training hard, and she knew her father would be waiting at the end of the 3.1 mile course. He was a cross country champion himself years ago in high school and college. She thought of her father's words, "Yes, winning is nice, but more importantly is to do your best, be fair, show good sportsmanship, and don't use excuses when you don't win."

The gun sounded and the runners sprinted off. Rachel, as planned, stayed in the middle of the pack as they neared the halfway point. She felt comfortable on this course as she had run it numerous times. She knew all the hills, curves, and sharp turns. At the two mile marker, she noticed that Cynthia Fergusen and several other girls strayed off course, instead of going straight. The wind had blown the direction sign down, and the lead runners thought the shortest route to the finish was to go off the trail and take a small shortcut. By going that way, the lead runners would shorten the race distance by nearly 200 yards. Rachel knew it would be almost impossible to make up that much distance in a championship race.

As Rachel glanced down at the fallen direction sign, she thought to herself, "If I go straight ahead and follow the proper trail, I'll never catch up, but if I go left and follow the others, that would be cheating, because we wouldn't cover the total 3.1 mile distance." She remembered the words her father said about being fair and not using excuses. She decided to go ahead and stay on the original course.

The group of lead runners eventually got back on course with less than a half mile to go. Rachel could see them from a distance. She picked up her pace and tried her best to catch up. Rachel was able to catch up, passing every runner but one, "Flash" Fergusen. Once again, Rachel finished second. Her father hugged her as a silver medal was placed around her neck.

Rachel never told her father about the girls, including Cynthia Fergusen, who took a major shortcut. In her heart, she knew she did the right thing by not cheating and by not coming up with excuses for finishing second. This event made her work and train harder than ever. She prepared for college competition.

Two years later, with her father in the stands, she crossed the finish line in first place, breaking the university's record time by almost 30 seconds! Rachel went on to be one of the best cross country runners in the nation. And...she never, ever told her father about the final race in her high school career. No excuses!

What would you have done if you were Rachel when she saw the others cheat and take a shortcut? It is so easy to go along with the crowd and do what they do, even when it is wrong. It takes more strength and character to do what is right, even if it means not finishing first. In the long run, people with good character are the real winners in life.

Always give your best and avoid the "loser's limp."

ACTIVITY 38:
Loser's Limp

Directions: During the next few weeks observe several games, sporting events on television or in person. Make a list of all the "loser's limps" you see.

Rachel's father encouraged her to always do her best and not to use excuses. Unfortunately excuses are heard often among athletes. *The umpire messed up. She cheated. The sun was in my eyes. He hit me first.* Seldom do you hear an athlete take the blame when things go wrong. Isn't it nice to hear a professional golfer tell a reporter after he missed a short putt, "It's my fault; I haven't been practicing my putting enough lately."?

In sports there is a term that is used often. It's called the "loser's limp." Watch a football, baseball, basketball game, a tennis match, or a track event and you'll probably see the "limp." It occurs like this:

A football player dives for the ball and misses. He gets up and limps back to the huddle. If he had caught the ball, you wouldn't see him limp.

In a track event the man in second knows he can't catch the leader, as he nears the finish line he pulls up with a limp. The winner seldom limps after he wins.

The "loser's limp" could also refer to other aspects of sports. For instance, the softball player drops the ball. What does she do next? She looks at the glove like it was the glove's fault that she couldn't catch the ball.

A baseball player strikes out and then stares at his bat!

A tennis player doesn't hit the ball well and glares at her racket.

The basketball player, Dennis Rodman has a foul called on him so he gives the referee a nasty glare.

LOSER'S LIMPS:

You Should Have Listened to Your Mother!

As I drank my morning coffee, I came across a timely article in the July 14, 1998 *USA Today* newspaper:

Willard, New Mexico: A 12 year-old boy who might have been trying to catch a rattlesnake was hospitalized after the snake struck him. Danny Keulen was bitten while playing outside his home and is in satisfactory condition.

People in the southwestern part of the United States like to tell amazing stories about the dangerous rattlesnake. The story that I am about to share with you centers on an often told legend of a mechanic's encounter with a large rattlesnake. Although I don't know the whole story I will share my version.

In a small town near the panhandle of Oklahoma, Jack, age 23, was eating dinner at his mother's house. He was an automobile mechanic at Berry's Garage, and he owned his own tow truck. The part of his job he enjoyed most was helping stranded travelers on the highway. Even as he ate dinner with his mom, he kept his beeper on just in case someone needed help.

As he was about to bite into a piece of peach pie, his beeper went off. A mother and her young child needed help. Their car had a flat tire and was pulled off the highway about three miles out of town.

Even though Jack was a young man, his mother still gave him daily advice. "Jack, don't forget to wear your safety equipment, especially your thick leather gloves!" Jack replied, "Okay Mom, I'll be back in an hour to finish the pie."

As he neared the stranded motorist, he noticed a rather large, wounded rattlesnake on the highway. Next to the snake was a fresh set of tire skid marks. This was not an uncommon site as snakes often sleep on the pavement at night to keep warm. Some drivers will run over a snake on purpose while others attempt to avoid it.

Jack parked his truck near the car. The lady told him that when she tried to avoid hitting the snake, her car began to spin and slid off the road, causing her flat tire. Jack informed her that she didn't miss the snake, she ran over it!

As he was removing the flat tire, he pricked his finger on something sharp. Maybe it was a nail stuck in the tire. It hurt and blood dripped from the finger. He thought to himself, "I should have listened to my mother and worn my safety gloves." A few minutes later the lady was on her way, and Jack headed back to his mother's house to finish his pie.

On his way home he began to get dizzy. His vision was blurry, and he had a hard time keeping the truck on the road. He passed out and his truck ran off the road into a wheat field.

After several hours Jack's mom became worried. She called her other son, Louis, to look for Jack. Louis traveled the roads near his mother's house until he found the truck in the field. When he opened the door, he found his brother Jack, dead.

It was days before doctors could determine the cause of Jack's death. When they investigated, the lady with the flat tire told police that Jack had hurt his finger while changing the tire. When the tire was examined, they found a large rattlesnake fang. Apparently when the lady ran over the snake, one of its fangs pulled off and stuck in the tire. When Jack took the tire off, he was cut by the fang, which released venom into his blood system causing him to die.

How often do you get angry or frustrated with your parents when they nag you about important things such as: "Be careful crossing the road," or "Don't run with sharp objects in your hand?" Your parents love you and remind you of things so you don't get hurt. If Jack had listened to his mother and worn his gloves, would he still be alive?

Believe it or not, your parents "nag" you because they love you.

ACTIVITY 39:
Agree or Disagree

Directions: You may not always agree with your parents. Here are a few quotes by famous people. Next to each one place an "A" if you agree with it or place "DA" next to it if you don't agree. Share your opinions/responses with other students.

> Often young people don't listen to their parents and they don't think they need to be hounded or constantly reminded about "little things." There may be times when you think you know more about life than your parents do. The older you get, the more your parents begin to make sense. Mark Twain noted, "When I was a boy of fourteen, my father was so ignorant I could barely stand to have the old man around. But when I got to be twenty-one, I was astonished at how much the old man had learned in seven years."

_______ 1. "As long as you can vision the fact that you can do something, you can do it—as long as you really believe it 100%." — ***Arnold Schwarzenegger***

_______ 2. "Kind words can be short and easy to speak but their echoes are truly endless." — ***Mother Teresa***

_______ 3. "You can turn painful situations around through laughter. If you can find humor in anything, even poverty, you can survive it." — ***Bill Cosby***

_______ 4. "It is easier to fight for one's principles than to live up to them." — ***Alfred Adler***

_______ 5. "A lie can travel halfway around the world while the truth is putting on its shoes." — ***Mark Twain***

_______ 6. "I never saw an instance of one or two disputants convincing the other by argument." — ***Thomas Jefferson***

_______ 7. "I destroy my enemy by making him my friend." — ***Abraham Lincoln***

_______ 8. "I have decided to stick with love. Hate is too great a burden to bear." — ***Martin Luther King, Jr.***

_______ 9. "Thinking is the hardest work there is, which is the probable reason why so few engage in it." — ***Henry Ford***

_______ 10. "Nothing pains some people more than having to think." — ***Martin Luther King, Jr.***

_______ 11. "People who fight fire with fire usually end up with ashes." — ***Abigail Van Buren***

_______ 12. "The most exhausting thing in life, I have discovered, is being insincere." — ***Anne Morrow Lindbergh***

Javier's Rabbits

Javier and his family moved from Monterrey, Mexico, to Los Angeles when he was only five years old. When he started kindergarten, he had a difficult time living in a new culture where he couldn't speak English. In school, he was often teased and fell behind in his schoolwork. Javier was small for his age, and by the time he reached third grade, kids started calling him names such as: midget, peewee, shorty, and stump. He felt he could never fit-in, and soon began to hate school. By the time he was sixteen, he dropped out.

Finding a good job was not easy without a high school diploma. For almost a year, he isolated himself from others. He stayed at home and never tried to make friends, and often complained about how cruel others were to him.

Eventually, at age seventeen, he got a job feeding animals at a science laboratory. His job was to feed rabbits, mice, rats, and other small animals that were being used for experiments. He did not like his job at first, but he realized that he was lucky to at least have an occupation to help support his family.

While working at the lab, several scientists were doing research on rabbits. The scientists put a group of rabbits on a diet rich in cholesterol. The rabbits were genetically comparable, so the scientists expected all of them to get blocked arteries at about the same rate — but they didn't. Some of the rabbits got a lot more blockage than others, and the scientists couldn't figure out why, since they were all on the same diet and they all had similar genes.

The rabbits were stacked in cages up to the ceiling. The ones in the higher cages were the rabbits that had more blockage and died sooner than the ones in the lower cages. At first, that made no sense. Why were the rabbits in the lower cages more healthy and living longer, even though they ate the same food? The puzzled scientists finally found the reason. They spent several days observing Javier as he fed the rabbits.

Because he was so short, he needed a ladder to feed the rabbits in the higher cages. Those rabbits were seldom touched, petted, picked up, or talked to. Javier concentrated his attention on the rabbits in the lower cages. He would often hold and play with them. He even spent his lunch hour playing with the privileged rabbits in the lower cages. He almost completely ignored the rabbits he couldn't reach without a ladder. The researchers wondered if Javier's special attention to the rabbits in the lower cages had an effect on their ability to live longer.

The scientists then did more studies. They again had Javier play, touch, and hold some rabbits, and ignore the others. Over and over again, the rabbits that got Javier's special attention continued to live longer than the ignored rabbits, even though they ate the same fatty, high cholesterol food. The researchers later published many articles in journals and magazines proving the importance of love and touch in helping animals and humans to live longer.

Javier himself learned a valuable lesson. He soon realized that instead of complaining and getting angry at other people because of the way they treated him, he began to be kind and caring towards others. The more he forgot his problems (being small, teased, and poor), the more he focused on helping others. And when he helped others feel good, he felt good too!

You have to love yourself before you can love others.

ACTIVITY 40:
Puppy Personalities

Directions: Javier learned that by being kind to his small group of rabbits, they were able to live longer, healthier lives than the rabbits that were ignored. Being kind to animals is as important as treating humans properly. How you raise, treat, handle animals when they are young will determine their personalities when they get older. The same is true for humans. Babies who are abused or neglected become adults who have trouble liking themselves and others.

Here is a story about three puppies. Read the story and answer the questions. Hopefully this activity will help to convince you that how animals are treated when they are young will determine their behaviors later in life.

Lonnie's Puppies

I visited my neighbor Lonnie. His German Shepherd had three beautiful puppies. They all came from the same mother and father dog and they all lived with their mother for 10 weeks before Lonnie put up a "Puppies for Sale" sign. All three puppies were fed well and Lonnie played with them daily. He sold the three puppies to three different families.

Six months later I decide to visit the three puppies to see how they are doing. I visit the Jones' who bought puppy A. As I drive up to the house the German Shepherd runs to see me. His tongue is hanging out as he greets me. I pet him for several minutes as he wags his tail. What a healthy, happy, gentle dog. I then visit the Hawkins' family to see puppy B. No one is home so I walk around looking for the dog. I find him under the porch. He is scared and nervous. He is skinny and will not let me get near him. As I try to pet him he starts shaking. Finally I travel to the Hughes' to check on puppy C. As soon as I get out of the truck the German Shepherd charges me. He is growling and trying to bite me. Luckily I got back into the truck before getting bitten. What a mean, aggressive dog!

1. How did puppy A become such a friendly, happy dog?

____

____

2. How did puppy B become so timid, scared, skinny, and nervous?

____

____

3. How did puppy C become so aggressive and mean?

____

____

Even Skunks Need Friends

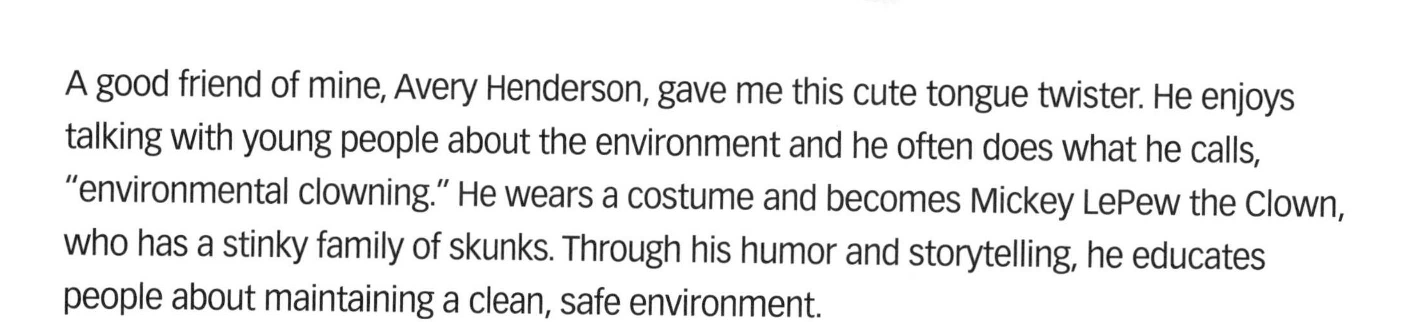

Try saying this three times, fast:

The skunk sat on the stump.
The stump thunk the skunk stunk,
And the skunk thunk the stump stunk.

A good friend of mine, Avery Henderson, gave me this cute tongue twister. He enjoys talking with young people about the environment and he often does what he calls, "environmental clowning." He wears a costume and becomes Mickey LePew the Clown, who has a stinky family of skunks. Through his humor and storytelling, he educates people about maintaining a clean, safe environment.

Everybody needs a friend, including the skunk. Avery Henderson could be considered one of their friends, but not too many other people mention the black, white-striped, bushy-tailed varmint as one of their favorite pets or animals. Recently, I did find another skunk lover, Donna Backus. I read about her in the newspaper.

Donna, a licensed wildlife rehabilitator, nurses injured animals at her house in Massachusetts. According to the newspaper article, Donna has seen an increase in the number of injured skunks being sent to her home. The reason for this is that the skunks, who love to visit town dumps and landfills, are getting their little heads caught in discarded Yoplait® yogurt cups. Generally, there's a little bit of yogurt in the container that attracts them. They are able to nudge their heads in. The Yoplait® container has a lip, which acts as a locking device on the animal's fur. When they try to go backwards, they can't get it off. They are unable to see, eat, drink, or breathe well. Then the helpless creatures spin around, slamming into buildings and bashing into trees. Wildlife experts say, that in about half the known cases, the skunks end up dying from suffocation, dehydration, or attacks by other animals.

People like Donna Backus and advocate groups like the Animal Protection Institute, decided to do something to help the skunk. They had to convince a huge company, General Mills, to redesign their Yoplait® containers. Most yogurt cups have a large opening at one end, and a lip that is turned inside-out so skunks cannot get trapped. But, the Yoplait's® cup has a small opening with the lip turned in. Could these people battle such a big company? Could they get them to invent a different style cup? Would a huge company spend thousands of dollars just to save a few skunks?

Thanks to the hard work of the skunk lover, General Mills has agreed to make some changes. The company is releasing a slightly altered, skunk-conscious design that has a wider top. Also, a warning label has been affixed to the bottom of each cup: "Protect Wildlife, Crush before Disposal."

Our younger generation needs to be very pro-active when it comes to protecting the environment. We will always need clean air, safe water to drink, beautiful trees, and our animals. I encourage young people to get involved and fight to not only "Save the Whale," but to support all of God's little creatures, including the not-so-popular skunk. Also, don't be afraid to challenge the government or huge companies. Talk with your political leaders and write letters to the appropriate people if you feel our animals or environment are being threatened. You can make a difference. Remember, a small group of people took on General Mills, a huge $6.8 billion corporation, to help save the skunk.

Be active in preserving our environment.

ACTIVITY 41:
An Invention Convention

Not too long ago, several fifth grade teachers at my school held an Invention Convention. Students were invited to create an invention. On the day of the convention they displayed their creations for parents and guests. Outside judges awarded ribbons to the winners.

In our story General Mills agreed to "invent" a new yogurt container for Yoplait®. Why not organize your own Invention Convention in your school or neighborhood? As you work on your entry be patient. You will probably make several mistakes and you'll get frustrated. You have to learn to fail and try again. Listen to what automotive inventor Charles Kettering, one of the 20th century's great creative minds, had to say about the value of learning to fail:

An inventor is simply a person who doesn't take his education too seriously. You see, from the time a person is six years-old until he graduates he has to take many examinations every year. If he flunks too often, he's out. But an inventor is almost always failing. He tries and fails maybe a thousand times. If he succeeds once then he's in. These two things are dramatically opposite. We often say that the biggest job we have is to teach a newly hired employee how to fail intelligently. We have to train him to experiment over and over and to keep on trying and failing until he learns what will work.

SUGGESTIONS FOR YOUR INVENTION CONVENTION:

1. Draw up a set of rules and guidelines.

2. Select a theme such as the environment, kitchen gadgets or space travel.

3. Invite people from your community to judge.

4. Contact the local newspaper for coverage.

5. Seek donations for ribbons and certificates.

Cal Ripken, Jr.'s Dilemma

Cal Ripken, Jr. is a remarkable athlete. On the evening of September 6, 1995, he broke Lou Gehrig's consecutive-games streak as he played in straight contest number 2,131 for the Baltimore Orioles. At the end of the 1998 baseball season, his streak passed 2,600 games! Cal played sixteen seasons in a row without missing a game! Although he seldom admits it, there were many days he wasn't feeling 100% and he was coping with minor injuries. To keep such a streak going, he not only had to avoid serious injury, but he also had to practice good sportsmanship so he wouldn't be suspended. Also, he constantly had to keep his fielding and hitting skills sharp in order to earn the right to be in the line-up for every game.

Cal knows that it takes not only hard work and great athletic ability to accomplish such a record. It also takes some luck. How did he avoid breaking a finger, spraining an ankle, getting hit in the head with a pitch, stubbing his toe in the bathtub, or missing an airplane flight for the next out-of-town game? Accidents happen, but he has been lucky to miss the serious ones.

Along his way to the major league record for consecutive-games played, he encountered one very serious dilemma. As he was nearing Lou Gehrig's record, his wife was ready to give birth to their second child. What if his wife Kelly went to the hospital to have the baby on the same day that he had a game? Would he forget about breaking the record and go to the hospital to be with his wife, or would he stay with the Orioles and continue the streak? Well, call it luck if you wish, but Kelly gave birth to a boy named Ryan on a day when the Orioles did not have a game scheduled! On his day off he was able to be with Kelly and Ryan.

I often wondered what would have happened if the Orioles had a game that day, and Cal chose to play baseball and not be with his wife. Would his reputation been tarnished? The answers to many of my questions about this event were answered while watching an interview with Cal on television. The reporter asked him the big question, "Cal, what would you have done if Ryan was born on a day when the Orioles had a game? Would you have played or went to the hospital, knowing your streak would end?"

Cal replied that he and his wife had given much thought to the situation. He noted that it was the toughest dilemma of his life. He told the reporter that he and Kelly agreed that if it happened on the day of a game, he would go the game and keep his streak alive. Some of you may be astonished and disappointed by this decision, but let me explain. Cal was not being arrogant or selfish; he was actually doing what he thought was best for Ryan. Cal told the reporter that when Ryan was old enough to understand the events of the past, then he might feel bad or guilty, knowing that his birth caused his dad to not break one of the greatest records ever in sports. Cal didn't want Ryan to suffer with any guilt. Later in life, would Ryan be questioned, teased, or constantly reminded that it was his birth that caused his father not to break the record?

Cal and Kelly spent hundreds of hours discussing the dilemma. They also talked with fiends, relatives, and even experts in the area of child-rearing. It was a decision that took a long time to make, and after much thought, the Ripken's believed they made the right choice.

Whenever you find yourself with a difficult decision to make, rely on the help and suggestions from others. Talk with your parents, teachers, good friends, and other people you trust. Take their advice, think about it for a few days, and then make the choice or decision that is best for you. Finally, don't make quick decisions on difficult dilemmas. Be patient, seek input, and you will probably be pleased with the results.

We all face dilemmas. Seek advice and support from those you respect.

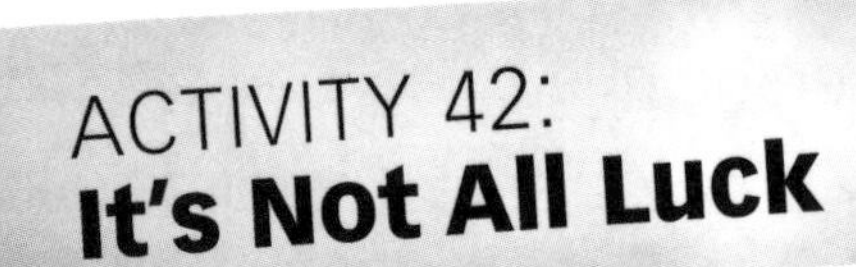

ACTIVITY 42:

It's Not All Luck

Directions: Ironman Cal Ripken, Jr. played major league baseball sixteen years in a row without missing a game. His consecutive-games streak is a record that probably will never be broken. Yes, he has been lucky in some aspects but, it took more than luck to accomplish such a feat.

By yourself, or in a group, see if you can list at least 20 things that Cal had to do or not do on his way to his remarkable record. You may use some of the ideas/items mentioned in the story.

---

1. ______________________
2. ______________________
3. ______________________
4. ______________________
5. ______________________
6. ______________________
7. ______________________
8. ______________________
9. ______________________
10. ______________________
11. ______________________
12. ______________________
13. ______________________
14. ______________________
15. ______________________
16. ______________________
17. ______________________
18. ______________________
19. ______________________
20. ______________________

The $912,825 Mistake

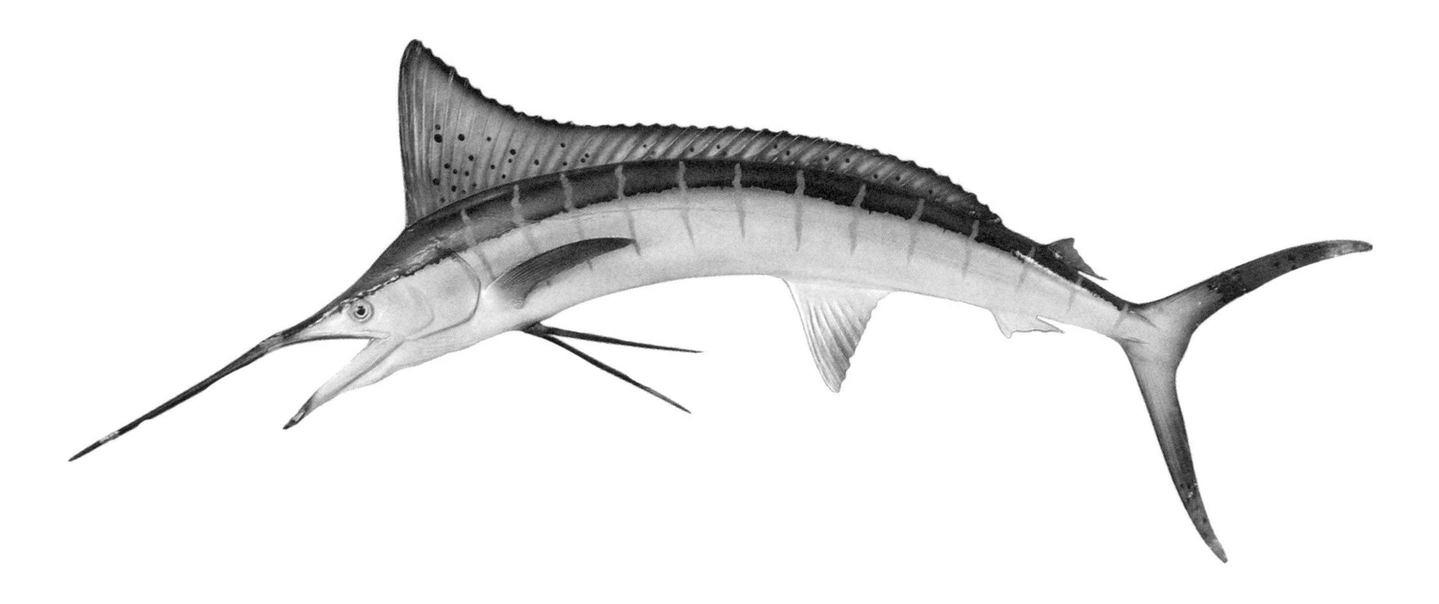

As long as you are breathing, you'll make mistakes. We all do. Nobody is flawless. One of the keys to success is to learn from our mistakes and hopefully avoid making the same mistake twice. Now some mistakes are easily fixed with an eraser, glue, or an apology, but some can cost us money. If you forget to pay your credit card on time you may have to pay a hefty large charge and your interest rate could go up. If you forget to get your car inspected, you might be issued a ticket by the police and have to pay a fine. If you forget to return books to the library on time you'll face an overdue fee. Most of these examples involve a small amount of money, but have you ever heard of a mistake that caused someone to lose over $900,000?

Captain Eric Holmes put together a top-notch crew on his boat Citation in preparation for the 2010 Big Rock Blue Marlin Fishing Tournament off the coast of North Carolina. $1.66 million in prize money was up for grabs. Holmes was confident he and his crew could finish first. One of his men, Andy Thomossan, caught a record 883-pound blue marlin on the first day of competition. The previous record for the largest blue marlin was 831 pounds. To everyone involved in the completion, it appeared that the Citation crew was going to win first place. For the remainder of the contest no other boat had a fisherman who could top Thomossan's catch.

Holmes and his men eagerly awaited the Saturday night awards banquet to claim their purse. Just before ceremony began Thomossan pulled his captain aside and said that the Citation had been disqualified. Holmes was dumbfounded. "What happened?" Thomossan responded, "One of our crew did not have a North Carolina fishing license." Under tournament rules "anyone fishing aboard a vessel" in the Big Rock Blue Marlin Fishing Tournament must have a valid North Carolina fishing license, including the captain, the mate, and anglers.

Since the Citation was disqualified the top prize of $912,825 went to the crew of the Carnivore. Angler John Parks caught what turned out to be the winner. It weight over 300 pounds less that Andy Thomossan's blue marlin! According to a news release, Thomossan said, "It hurts. No record. No Money. No fish. No nothing. Yep, it's a nice ending to the story, isn't it?"

Someone on Holmes' boat made a mistake. He forgot to get a license. A North Carolina Coastal Recreational License costs only $15 annually for state residents 16 and older or $30 for non-residents, according to the N.C. Department of Environment and Natural Resources website. A 10-day license can be purchased for $5 for state residents 16 and older or $10 for nonresidents. So, basically, the lack of a $15 fishing license cost the Citation $912,825. What a mistake!

What would you say to the rest of the crew if you were the guilty party? If you were on the Citation what would you say to the member who failed to secure his license? Could you forgive him? Whoever the forgetful fisherman was, I bet he doesn't forget his license for the next Big Rock Blue Marlin Fishing Tournament!

Don't overlook the little things in life.

ACTIVITY 43:
One mistake can lead to another.

Directions: We all make mistakes, little one and big ones. It is important to correct our mistakes as soon as we can or bigger mistakes may follow. Often our mistakes can affect others. Read the following story that shows how one mistake can lead to others. Then get creative to make up a story of your own. Keep the "Domino Theory" in mind. Remember, just like one domino falls over and knocks down the next, our actions impact others.

Nine year-old Benny forgot to lock the gate and his dog Max got out. Max ran across the highway. A car driven by Mr. Johnson saw Max coming so he swerved off the road to avoid hitting him. Now Mr. Johnson' car is in the ditch. He calls for help and got to work two hours late. On that morning Mr. Johnson was supposed to ship out five boxes of computers to a major client. Because he was late, the computers were not delivered on time. Mr. Johnson was fired! Because he was fired he was so sad that he forgot that he was to be at an evening gathering to see his brother receive a very special award. His brother, Jim was angry that he wasn't there. After the scout meeting Jim stopped at a diner and was rude to a waitress named Minnie. Now Minnie is upset and fusses at a co-worker named Jill. Jill cries and leaves. Because the diner is now one waitress short, service is slow. Mrs. Jones, a customer gets poor service and tells the manager, Mr. Schmidt that she'll never come back. Now Mr. Schmidt is upset and goes home and fusses at his teenage daughter, Serena.

Here's my story.

"Help – The Pelican's got My Dog"

Every time I try to tell this story, I break out in a loud laugh. I wish I could have witnessed this actual event. Now don't get me wrong, I love dogs, but what happened to this little Chihuahua was a bit scary and yet, very funny.

Mrs. Billings owned a miniature Chihuahua named Pebbles. The very small dog weighed less than two pounds and could be held in the palm of your hand. She had the dog for over ten years. One day, Mrs. Billings, her daughter Annie, and Pebbles went to the beach. Along the way they stopped at a convenience store to pick up a few supplies. The store's owner was an old sailor who joked to Mrs. Billings about being careful at the beach with her little dog. He told her, "The sea gulls and pelicans would love to gobble him up!"

Later in the day, Mrs. Billings decided to take a short nap under her beach umbrella. She tells Annie to keep an eye on Pebbles. Annie begins to build a rather large sand castle. She becomes so involved in her project that she forgets about Pebbles. The dog is playing at the edge of the water.

A few minutes later Annie hears another person on the beach yell, "Look, the pelican is trying to get the dog!" After two or three attempts, a large Brown Pelican scooped up the Chihuahua and began to fly away. Annie screams and wakes her mom. Both of them start running along the beach yelling to the bird to bring their dog back. Later, it was discovered that another person on the beach at that time, had a video camera and filmed the event. The film showed the little dog hanging in the pelican's pouch and looking out between the beak. Pebbles did not seem the least bit concerned.

Back on the ground, many more people were now running after the bird, yelling at it, and throwing things. The pelican finally dropped the dog in the sand. When Mrs. Billings approached the "grounded" dog, she thought it was dead because it was not moving. Finally, Pebbles got up. He only had the wind knocked out of him. Once her beloved little pooch was okay, she started fussing at Annie for not keeping an eye on the dog as she had been told. The more she was scolded, the more she cried. Later that day when things had settled down, Mrs. Billings apologized to Annie for yelling at her, and Annie in return, said, "I'm sorry, too!"

There is a good lesson to be learned from this story (besides keeping your Chihuahua away from pelicans). Many events happen in a family that cause emotions to run high, and some of these events are retold many years later and viewed as funny. When the pelican had the dog, Mrs. Billings was yelling and fussing at Annie. She was quite upset. Years from now they will retell this story numerous times and they will laugh.

When you do something very wrong or dangerous, your parents /guardians will get upset with you, and if necessary, punish or discipline you. They do this because they love you and don't want you to get hurt. For instance, maybe you were trying to cook something on the stove and a fire started. You get yelled at and sent to your room. When you become an adult, your dad will laugh as he tells the story about how you almost burned the house down while cooking eggs.

Part of growing up is learning and making mistakes. If your parents /guardians seem to over-react or make a big deal over something that you think is really not that important, take your punishment and listen to their mini-sermon. They get very emotional because they do care about you. Remember, your misdeeds or accidents today, will make great conversation and bring a few smiles as the years go by.

"No mind is thoroughly well organized that it is deficient in a sense of humor."
— S.T. Coleridge

ACTIVITY 44:
Humor is Contagious

Directions: We all need to laugh often and even get a bit silly. One way to have a chuckle or two is to tell a joke or attempt to solve a silly puzzle. Here is a puzzle that is adapted from the book, *Are You Smart or What?* Match each word in the left-hand column with a silly definition in the right-hand column. To have a few laughs, solve this puzzle with the help of a friend or two. The answers are in the back of the book.

A. arbitrator	1. a clumsy ophthalmologist
B. avoidable	2. what trees do in the spring
C. burglarize	3. quitting Arby's to work at McDonald's
D. eyedropper	4. what to do to relax your wife
E. heroes	5. what a seafood store owner does
F. baloney	6. what a bullfighter does
G. pharmacist	7. what a guy in a boat does
H. relief	8. where some hemlines fall
I. rubberneck	9. a helper on a farm
J. selfish	10. what a crook sees with

The Legendary "Goat"

AN OBITUARY — *USA TODAY* • APRIL 22, 1998

Earl "The Goat" Manigault, the legendary New York City playground basketball player whose descent into heroin addiction cost him a professional career, died Friday of congestive heart failure in New York. Manigault, whose life was made into a 1996 HBO movie was 53. The six foot, one inch Manigault was "the best player of his size in the history of New York City," according to NBA Hall of Famer, Kareem Abdul-Jabbar, who often squared off against "The Goat" in parks during the 1960's. But while city contemporaries such as Abdul-Jabbar and Connie Hawkins went on to pro careers, Manigault battled drug problems. The drugs sapped his abilities and he failed a 1971 tryout with the ABA Utah Stars. His stunts were legendary:

- leaping to place a quarter atop a backboard
- reverse-dunking a basketball 36 times to win a $60 bet
- Author Pete Axthelm, in his book, *The City Game*, said "The Goat" would occasionally drive past a few defenders, dunk the ball with one hand, catch it with the other, and raise it and stuff it through the hoop a second time before returning to earth.

After starting at Harlem's Benjamin Franklin High School, he went to a prep school in Laurinburg, North Carolina, and attracted major college recruiters. But he opted for Johnson C. Smith College where his grades plunged, and he fought with his coach over playing time. He returned to Harlem's playgrounds and later served 16 months in jail for drug possession in 1969-1970, and another term from 1977-1999 in a failed robbery plot. Manigault eventually kicked his habit and came back to Harlem as a community activist. He began working in a neighborhood recreation and counseling center for teens. He became an unofficial coach at Wadleigh High, which won this year's city title.

What a story this obituary tells! Earl had the potential to become one of the greatest players ever in the National Basketball Association. His name could have been as recognizable as Larry Bird, Michael Jordan, Karl Malone, Magic Johnson, or Wilt Chamberlain, but as the newspaper noted, "drugs sapped his abilities." His addiction to drugs messed up his family, his career as a basketball player, and it shortened his life. Hopefully, Earl's story will prevent other young people from falling into the drug scene. Luckily, "The Goat" was able to spend the last few years of his life working with young people, in hopes that they would stay straight.

You don't need drugs to get high. You can feel great and get high on life by helping others, doing well in school, playing sports, taking interest in art or music, or getting involved in a religion of your choice. Having character is the ability to stay away from negative influences in life such as alcohol, drugs, and smoking. By keeping busy in positive activities and practicing good character, you will be successful.

I finish this story with a quote by Sid Simon. This well-known author, psychologist, and college professor once said, "If I really like myself then I won't do anything to hurt myself or others." I agree with him. If you do feel good about yourself, then you don't need drugs, and the truth is — drugs can hurt you and others!

Everyday do something to improve yourself.

ACTIVITY 45:
Our Obituary

Directions: Earl "The Goat" Manigault lived to be only 53 years-old. When you read his obituary from the newspaper you'll note that he had great athletic ability and in his later years did make an attempt to coach and counsel troubled youth.

As you know, we all must die someday but, let's hope we live to be a healthy 100 years-old! When we eventually die, our obituary will end up in the local newspaper. Let's pretend that you do live to be 100. Write your own obituary below. Be sure not to forget about some of your personal characteristics (i.e., hard-working, honest, kind, etc.) as well as your accomplishments. Mention a few things about your family and your hobbies.

Newtown Morning News Obituary

Person: ______________________________

Born: ______________________________

Died: ______________________________

____

____

____

____

____

____

____

____

____

The Toothpaste Theory

Quite often I have teachers and parents ask me, "How do you motivate young people?" I tell them, "With words." I believe words can be the biggest motivators or de-motivators for almost everyone. Kind, positive words help others to feel good, appreciated, welcome, and energized. Mean, sarcastic comments hurt and anger others. Seldom do others forget the positive or negative comments we make. When you tease someone and call them fat or ugly, they don't forget. When you tell your teacher, "Thanks, I appreciate your help," he/she won't forget. Very hurtful comments and very positive comments directed at us will be remembered for many years.

One of my favorite classroom lessons is, "The Toothpaste Theory." It is a valuable strategy I use to help students realize the importance of being careful about what they say to others. I bring a large toothbrush and tube of toothpaste to class. I then squeeze a big glob of toothpaste onto the brush. Next, I say to the class, "I don't think I'll brush my teeth now. Can I get all the toothpaste back into the tube?" Of course, most students tell me, "No, you can't get all the paste back into the small hole. Some will stick to the brush, and some will spill onto the outside of the tube, and you'll get some on your fingers!"

I agree with the students and tell them, "Yes, it is impossible to get all the paste back into the tube. The same goes for words that you say. Once you say something, it is impossible to put your words back into your mouth." So be careful what you say.

When you are angry, take a few deep breaths before responding. If you do say something unkind, apologize.

Here is a cute story that helps prove my point about the power of words. Jaime Escalante, the high school teacher upon whom the movie, "Stand and Deliver," was based, told this story about a fellow teacher. The teacher had two students named Johnny. One was a happy child, an excellent student, and a fine citizen. The other Johnny spent much of his time goofing off and making a nuisance of himself. When the PTA held its first meeting of the year, a mother came up to this teacher and asked, "How's my son Johnny getting along?" He assumed she was the mom of the better student, and replied, "I can't tell you how much I enjoy him. I'm so glad he's in my class."

The next day the problem child came to the teacher and said, "My mom told me what you said about me last night. I haven't had a teacher who wanted me in his class." That day he completed his assignments and brought in his completed homework the next morning. A few weeks later, the "problem Johnny" had become one of the teacher's hardest working students, and one of his best friends. This misbehaving child's life was turned around all because he was mistakenly identified as a good student.

According to Escalante, "Not every lazy or underachieving boy or girl could be motivated by a simple compliment from a teacher, of course, but there is a principle here that applies to all kids. It's better to make a child stretch to reach your high opinion, than to stoop to match your disrespect."

Words are the biggest motivators and de-motivators of people.

ACTIVITY 46:
It's not what you say; it's how you say it.

Directions: There's a lot of truth to the statement, "It's not what you say; it's how you say it." For instance, take this statement, "I don't like what you just said to me." If you say it one way you come across as angry. If you say it another way, without changing the words, you can sound sad.

Get with a partner and take turns reading the following statements. Then, without changing the words, read the statements with different emotions. Say the statements in ways that may sound angry, sad, jealous, boastful, sarcastic, and so on.

Where did you get that silly looking shirt?

Why don't you leave me alone?

I got a higher test score than you.

I hope you have a great day.

I'm not going to work today.

I don't care if he beats me in the race today.

You should have practiced more.

I'm not ugly.

I don't want to do that.

I Promise to Pay You Back

It was a June evening in a small town in Alabama. Nearly 200 people gathered in the high school's cafeteria for a special celebration. After forty years of work for the school, Henry Willis was retiring. Friends, co-workers, and family members sat as he approached the podium. Hank, as he was called by everyone in school, was well-loved. He missed only six days of work in those forty years, and he won numerous awards. Most employees retire when they are 60 or 65, but Hank worked until the age of 72, because as he said, "I put six children through college and I couldn't retire until their expenses were paid!"

As he addressed the audience, he thanked them for all their love and support over the years. There were tears in his eyes as he looked back over his career. As he neared the end of his speech, he told the group about his most memorable experience. Everyone sat quietly and listened to his remarkable story.

"About fifteen years ago, a boy named Tony moved here in ninth grade. He lived with his great-grandmother. Because of her age and poor health, she could barely raise the young boy. He often came to school without a coat or lunch money. He had no one at home to help him with his schoolwork, and he was pretty isolated from friends on weekends and in the summer, because his great-grandmother could not drive. I took a liking to the lad."

Hank continued, "During his four years here, I helped him the best I could. I let him help me clean up after school so he could earn some money. Although I didn't read too well myself, I did try to help him with homework. He would tell me about his wish to go to Alaska someday, and I told him of my dream of taking my wife to Hawaii

when I retire. Because he was always broke, he asked me for money. Sometimes I gave him a quarter for ice cream, and once I even gave him fifty dollars to cover graduation expenses. Tony would always tell me, 'I promise to pay you back someday.' It wasn't until I cleaned out my office about a month ago that I found all of Tony's promissory notes in the bottom drawer of my desk. There were 34 notes totaling over $200. He signed and dated each one and wrote, 'I promise to pay you back someday.' On graduation day, I wished him good luck and told him he didn't owe me a dime, but again he gave me his promise to pay me back. A week after graduation, his great-grandmother died, and he had to move to Philadelphia to live with his uncle. I had not heard a thing from Tony until I got this letter last week." He opened the letter and started reading.

Dear Hank,

Congratulations on your retirement. I apologize for not writing or calling you sooner. In fact, for a couple of years I became so involved in making money, that I totally forgot about the days in high school. I am a very successful car salesman in Arlington, Virginia. I'm married and have two girls. Last year, I won an award for being the top salesperson in our district and received a free trip to Alaska. My dream came true. Recently, I found out I'd won another trip. As my manager told me I was going to Hawaii, something strange happened. When I saw the pictures of Hawaii, I thought of you. I realized that even though I am doing well now, there were many people like you who helped me along the way. Hank, you helped me the most. I remember the many times I borrowed money from you, the times you helped me with homework, and I probably wouldn't have graduated without your support. But, what I remember the most were our dreams of Alaska and Hawaii. My dream came true and now I want your dream to come true. I told my manager to send you and your wife the award package I won. It includes free airline tickets to Hawaii, hotel reservations and extra expense money. You're going to Hawaii! I promised to pay you back. Now you can mark my account, PAID IN FULL!
Thank you for everything. Have a great retirement.

—Tony Garner

Keeping your promises builds trust and respect.

ACTIVITY 47: Three Thank You Letters, Today!

When was the last time you thanked someone for helping you? Have you ever written a "Thank you" note to a teacher, parent, baby sitter, or coach? Everyone enjoys receiving kind words of appreciation and when you thank others, you actually feel better as well.

Forget about the telephone, texting, and computer. Instead, take out three sheets of paper and write three letters to three different, important people in your life. Don't forget about your past teachers. Let all these people know that you appreciate them and that they made a difference in your life.

Put the letters in envelopes and mail them today!

Women can't run a marathon!

A few years ago *USA Today* had an article about the ten hardest things to do in sports. According to the article, 'running a marathon' was one of the ten. An official marathon distance is 26.2 miles. Over the years I have completed fifteen of them, so I know how difficult the race can be. Nowadays there are hundreds of marathons taking place in the United States and the most prestigious of them is the Boston Marathon. Runners have to have a 'qualifying' time in another marathon in order to run in Boston. I have yet to qualify but my son has; he has run the Boston Marathon three times!

In the early years of marathoning it was solely an event for men. Women were not allowed to participate, but oh how things have changed! Today you'll find almost as many women as men competing in these long distance races. What triggered these changes? Let me tell you about Roberta Gibb and Katherine Switzer. Thanks to their hard work, determination, and risk-taking, women today are well-respected in the world of running.

Roberta (Bobbi) Gibb: Bobbi was a great artist who also loved to run. Almost every day before she began painting she would go for a long run. She heard about a race called the Boston Marathon so she started serious training. She logged all her miles in a journal. One day she actually ran forty miles. She submitted her application for the race. She continued to train awaiting her acceptance letter. When the letter came, it contained bad news. Her application was denied based on these three Boston Marathon rules in 1966:

1. Women were not allowed.
2. Women were not physiologically capable of running 26.2 miles.

3. The longest running distance for women sanctioned by the Amateur Athletic Union was one and a half miles.

Despite being rejected, she still drove to Boston. On the day of the race she hid in the bushes near the starting line. She borrowed her brother's running shorts and covered her upper body with a hooded sweatshirt. When the gun sounded she joined the men. Although she was an 'unofficial' participant, she ran the course in 3 hours and 21 minutes and finished ahead of two-thirds of the men! It wasn't until thirty years later that the Boston Athletic Association gave her credit for being the female winner of the 1966 race.

Katherine Switzer: In 1967 Katherine tried a different strategy for the event than the one used by Gibb the previous year. Switzer knew her application would also be denied based on the fact that she was a woman. So, when she filled out her application she listed her name as "K. V. Switzer." The race officials assumed the name must be a male so she received her official bib and race number in the mail. On race day she did her best to dress like a man. She put her long hair under her hat and put on her racing bib. She took off running with the sound of the starting gun. About half way through the race, the director found out there was a woman in the race. When he finally spotted Katherine he yelled at her and told her to get off the course. Her boyfriend pushed the director aside and Katherine continued. Once the spectators saw a woman in the race they cheered her on. She eventually made it to the finish line. Bobbi Gibb ran that day as well, but without an official race number and bib. She finished an amazing one hour ahead of Switzer.

One of my favorite quotes is "If you want something you've never had, you must do something you've never done." Gibb and Switzer wanted something they never had: the opportunity to prove women could complete in marathons. To prove it they had to do something they hadn't done before: train hard and take a risk.

Everyone needs a hero.

ACTIVITY 48:
Four Heroes

Katherine Switzer and Bobbi Gibb are heroes to many female athletes who were told they couldn't perform as well as men. Who are your heroes? I attended a conference one year where a presenter noted that we all need four heroes:

- **A present day hero:** This is someone who is alive today that you don't know personally. He or she could be an athlete, politician, singer, actor, author, artist, etc.
- **A historical hero:** This would be someone not alive today. It could be a former president, explorer, writer, author, athlete or someone else you've admired.
- **A personal hero:** This would be someone you know personally that has had a big impact on your life. It could be one of your parents, a teacher, a coach, or scout leader.
- **A biblical hero:** Select one of your favorite characters from the bible.

MY PRESENT DAY HERO IS ______________________________

Because ______________________________

____

MY HISTORICAL HERO IS ______________________________

Because ______________________________

____

MY PERSONAL HERO IS ______________________________

Because ______________________________

____

MY BIBLICAL HERO IS ______________________________

Because ______________________________

____

Today or Tomorrow?

Have you ever noticed how often people say that they will begin or stop doing something tomorrow? They are always putting things off until tomorrow. "I'll stop smoking tomorrow." "I'll start my diet tomorrow." "Pretty soon I'll start studying more so my grades go up." "One of these days I'll visit my uncle in the hospital."

We need to stop putting things off, because tomorrow may be too late! In his book, *Living, Loving, and Learning*, Leo Buscaglia tells of a teenage girl who wrote a poem about putting things off. The poem centers around her boyfriend who went off to war. Maybe we all can learn a lesson from her.

Things You Didn't Do

***Remember the day I borrowed your brand new car and I dented it?
I thought you'd kill me, but you didn't.***

And remember the time I dragged you to the beach, and you said it would rain, and it did? I thought you'd say, "I told you so." But you didn't.

Do you remember the time I flirted with all the guys to make you jealous, and you were? I thought you'd leave me, but you didn't.

***Do you remember the time I spilled strawberry pie all over your car rug?
I thought you'd hit me, but you didn't.***

And remember the time I forgot to tell you the dance was formal and you showed up in jeans? I thought you'd drop me, but you didn't.

Yes, there were lots of things you didn't do. But you put up with me, and you loved me, and you protected me. There were lots of things I wanted to make up to you when you returned from Vietnam. But you didn't.

A few weeks after reading this poem for the first time, something happened in my family that made me realize the importance of not putting things off. My son, Aaron, age ten at the time, was hit by a car that was traveling fifty miles an hour. He was flipped over and the car landed in the middle of a busy highway. He was in critical condition as he was rushed off to the hospital. I spent several hours in the emergency room waiting to hear his condition from the doctor. As I sat there, not knowing if he would live or die, I began to think of all the promises I had made him and all the things we were planning to do together. Luckily, he survived and he is a healthy young man. From that point on, I began spending more time with him. When he would say, "Let's throw the football around," I didn't say, "No, I'm busy, maybe tomorrow."

Starting today, make a pledge to yourself to stop putting things off until tomorrow. Set some goals, write them down, get support from others, and begin! Now!

ACTIVITY 49: Important Things to Do

Directions: One of the best ways to get things done is to write a plan. A good plan should include a what, a how, and a when. What is your plan? How are you going to do it? When are you going to do it?

For instance, your plan may be to learn how to play the piano. So your plan might include:

What: To learn how to play the piano good enough to do a song in church.
How: To practice every Monday, Wednesday, and Friday from 3-5pm.
When: To practice on these days and times for three months so I'll be ready to play at the Christmas Program on December 17.

Suggestions for writing your plan:

1. Write your plan on a piece of paper and post it somewhere so that you'll see it often.
2. Share your plan with others and ask for their support. Tell them to check-up on you once in awhile to make sure you are doing what you said you would.
3. Set realistic goals.
4. Don't accept excuses!
5. Don't give up. If your plan fails, try again.
6. Be patient. Some goals take a little longer to reach.

MY PLAN

What: ______________________________

How: ______________________________

____

When: ______________________________

Date: ______________________________

Signature: ______________________________

Co-Signer/buddy: ______________________________

El Nino and the Happy Cats

Throughout the world, 1998 will go down in history as one of the craziest years ever for weather. There were plenty of droughts, heat waves, floods, forest fires, tornadoes, and powerful hurricanes. Most people put the blame on a unique weather pattern called, El Nino. El Nino has been blamed for such things as behavior changes in people, and the increase in the number of mosquitoes. The bad weather has caused many to suffer, but I know one group that is smiling — the cats in Vietnam.

Let me explain. Thanks to El Nino, a severe draught hit the country of Vietnam, causing hungry rodents to gnaw their way through rice paddies, granaries, and storage bins all across southeast Asia. The rat and mice reproduction rates were so high that the government had to intervene. Local officials offered a cash bounty of 2.5 cents for each rat tail brought in, newspapers were encouraging schoolchildren to flush out as many of the pesky critters as they could, and beat them to death with sticks. Farmers were advised to string electrical wire around their fields, and zookeepers in Hanoi released snakes from cages.

The most controversial move came from Vietnam's Prime Minister, Phan Van Khai's decree aimed at increasing the number of natural rat predators by outlawing the consumption of cats. That's right. Until the rat problem was under control, no one was allowed to eat cats, in a country that loved to dine on feline! Every week, tens of thousands of tabbies end up in cooking pots. Fancy restaurants often serve roast cat, a dish so prized the connoisseurs were willing to fork over $40 for a black tabby with a long tail and short, succulent legs! Restaurant owners had to tell angry customers, "Sorry, these days we cannot serve cat, it's against the law."

In the United States, we would never think of eating cute, furry, lovable cats. Just the thought sickens me, but in some countries they are considered tasty treats. While El Nino was bad news for most, it was good news for cats living in Vietnam!

There is a valuable lesson to learn from this story - what is considered bad news for one person could be good news for someone else. For example, if the roof on your home blows off during a storm, that's bad news for you, but good news for men who make a living fixing roofs. El Nino may have increased the number of bugs around your house, but that is good news for the Orkin man.

Another point here, is that even terribly bad, scary, and traumatic events can cause good things to happen. A family may lose their home in a fire, and then later realize how important their neighbors and churches are in their lives as they are given food, money, love, support, and even physical help to rebuild. You may have been saddened by the loss of a pet, only to get another one that you love even more than the first one.

So remember…when something unfortunate happens, hang in there. If you survive a bad event, be patient — good things will reward you in the future.

When bad things happen, be patient.
Often good things follow.

ACTIVITY 50:
El Nino...The Good and Bad

Directions: The El Nino weather pattern of 1998 caused much hardship for people because of droughts, floods, fires, tornadoes, and hurricanes. Remember from the story, often when bad things happen, good things can follow. Below are two columns. In column one list at least ten "bad things" that happened to people because of El Nino. In column two list at least ten "good things" that took place because of the bad weather. You may use some of the examples in the story.

THE BAD NEWS	THE GOOD NEWS
1. ______________	______________
2. ______________	______________
3. ______________	______________
4. ______________	______________
5. ______________	______________
6. ______________	______________
7. ______________	______________
8. ______________	______________
9. ______________	______________
10. ______________	______________

A Roy Rogers Reputation

Have you ever heard of the famous Roy Rogers? If you haven't, ask one of your parents/guardians. Roy Rogers was one of the first television cowboy stars, and singing cowboys in motion pictures. His television show was full of action as he lived on a ranch with his wife, Dale Evans, and his horse, Trigger. He almost always caught the bad guys, and his show ended with Roy and his wife singing "Happy Trails To You." To many youngsters, Roy was a real hero.

Roy died at the age of 86. A few days after his death, I was watching a tribute to him on television. The host of the show mentioned that most famous movie stars, singers, or athletes at one time or another have been guilty of getting in trouble with the law, involved in drugs, or doing some other not-so-moral thing. When the host and others on the show started talking about Roy's life, no one could think of anything negative to say about him. He was honest, hard-working, faithful to his wife, very Christian, didn't smoke or drink alcohol, and he was always donating his time and money to help others.

Roy had what some call, a great reputation. If you look up the word "reputation" in the dictionary, you'll see words like: a general opinion or impression, good character, good report, having a good name, of high repute.

Now, when I talk with young people, I use the term "A Roy Rogers Reputation," meaning to use good character, doing what is right and legal, and having others respect you. Everyone has a reputation that can be considered good or bad. A reputation takes a long time to develop. For instance, if a new boy moved into your

neighborhood, how would you know if you could trust him? It will take several days or even months before you can begin to determine his character.

Have you ever asked yourself, "What is my reputation?" What if some of your past teachers were talking about you? What would they be saying? However they describe you, they will describe your reputation. A good reputation can help you, while a bad reputation can hurt you. If you have the habit of being honest, then you have a good chance of getting a job at the school store. If you have a history of cheating or stealing, then you probably won't get the job.

Here is an example of how Jenny's reputation helped her — and how Bob's reputation hurt him. Both students are in Mrs. Burton's fifth grade class. On Monday of the last week of school, Mrs. Burton tells her class that the last homework assignment of the year is to do a science project and turn it in on Thursday. All year, Jenny has never failed to complete an assignment. She always has her homework done with no excuses. Bob almost never does homework, and he always made up wild stories about why he didn't get it done.

On the day that Mrs. Burton gave the last homework assignment, Jenny went home and completely forgot about it. It wasn't until she got on the school bus Thursday morning, that she remembered, but it was too late. She never got it done!

On the day that Mrs. Burton gave the last homework assignment, Bob went straight home and started on his project. He was determined to do an excellent job, because he could use an "A" on the project to help him pass science. For three evenings he worked hard on the assignment. He didn't go out to play or watch television. On Thursday morning, he got up early and put his project in the back seat of the car. He knew Mrs. Burton would be proud of him, and that she would give him a good grade. Bob's mom drove him to school. He got out of the car and she drove away quickly, as she had an important meeting in a city eighty miles away. When he entered the school building, he remembered his project that he left in the car. By the time he returned to the parking lot, his mother was gone.

Jenny didn't do her homework, but she told Mrs. Burton she had. Bob told his teacher about his super project and how he had accidentally left it in the back seat of his mother's car. Who was telling the truth, Jenny or Bob? Who will Mrs. Burton believe?

ACTIVITY 51: Reputations

Directions: Roy Rogers will always be remembered as a well-respected man with a near perfect reputation. Here are some questions concerning reputations. Share your responses with others.

1. Can you think of some people (living or dead) who you feel had/have good reputations?

___

2. Can you think of other well-known personalities who had/have questionable reputations?

___

3. How long does it take to form a positive reputation? ___

4. How long does it take to build a bad reputation? ___

5. Talk to other students and see if you can find someone famous that you disagree on their reputation. For example, you may think that Tiger Woods has a bad reputation but a friend may disagree.

___

6. If several of your teachers and neighbors got together to talk about you, what would they say? Would their words be positive or would their words be very critical? How they describe you is their perception of you as a person (your reputation).

___

7. What two characteristics about yourself would you like to change for the better?

___ ___

8. Can someone have a good reputation and still "mess-up" once in awhile? ❑ YES ❑ NO

9. What are some advantages of having a good reputation?

___

10. How can a bad reputation hurt you?

___

Why can't you be more responsible?

"Why can't you be more responsible?" Throughout his middle and high school years Justin must have heard his parents ask that question a hundred times. Justin was a very likeable, yet quirky kid and his parents were constantly frustrated with him because he was always losing things or forgetting to do things. He seldom made excuses. He always apologized for not being responsible and promised to try harder the next time. At times his mother and father felt bad for fussing at him so much.

There was the time Justin came home from school barefooted. "Justin," mom shouted, "Where are the new sneakers we bought you?" Justin replied, "I don't know. I must have left them at school." Another time he came home from school on a very cold day without his jacket. "Justin, where is your new coat?" As always Justin replied, "I don't know." During the first week of school in his sophomore year he told his dad that he needed to buy some more school supplies. "We just spent fifty dollars on supplies last week. What did you do with them?" his father asked. "I don't know" was Justin's regular reply. His mother noticed that there were many days when Justin rushed straight to the kitchen after school to stuff his face with junk food.

Mom would say, "Didn't you eat anything for lunch at school?" Justin would often say, "No, I lost my lunch money."

His parents continued to preach to him about the importance of being a responsible young adult. They even considered referring him for counseling. Then tragedy hit. The day before the start of his junior year in high school Justin was killed in a car accident. The school held a memorial service. His parents were stunned to see hundreds show up. They thought Justin was a loner with few friends. One by one students spoke about how kind and generous Justin had been.

One boy talked about the day he came to school with a ragged old pair of sneakers that were totally worn out. The boy told Justin that he couldn't get a new pair for at least a month until his dad's social security check came. Justin gave him his new pair and walked home barefooted. Then there was a young girl who cried as she recalled the day Justin gave her his jacket as she shivered at the bus stop. A boy named Juan told a story how Justin saw him sitting in the cafeteria with no food. Justin asked him why he wasn't eating and Juan told him that the cafeteria lady wouldn't let him charge any more money. Justin gave Juan his lunch money. Jasmine remembered the day Justin caught her crying outside the history classroom. Jasmine told Justin that she was afraid to go inside because the teacher would embarrass and humiliate her because she didn't have the correct notebook for note-taking. Justin gave her his notebook.

As the stories continued, Justin's parents were no longer crying. They began to smile. They were proud of their son. They now realized that he wasn't irresponsible, he was kind. He was willing to make sacrifices to help others. They remember a quote by George Eliot, "What do we live for, if not to make life less difficult for each other?"

Responsibilities and privileges increase with age.

ACTIVITY 52:

The older you get, the more responsibilities you get

Directions: In one family there are three children ages 6, 12, 18. Under each column list as many responsibilities as you can think of that a child of that age would have. After you complete your lists, buddy up and compare lists.

AGE 6	AGE 12	AGE 18

From Bullies to Burgers

My favorite day of the year is Christmas Eve. There always seems to be a special feeling in the air on that day. Even though people are hustling around, finding those last-minute gifts, visiting friends, and preparing to cook, they smile at strangers and seem to be more kind and polite than usual. Many of us have good memories of things happening on that special evening. As a child I was always allowed to open one present on Christmas Eve before going to bed. Of course, I didn't get much sleep after that, wondering what other gifts Santa might bring.

Even though many nice things happen at that time of the year, there is still a criminal element roaming the streets. Unfortunately, statistics find that robbery, child abuse, and alcohol related crimes are very prevalent during the holiday season. Although most everyone is kind, generous, and happy, we need to remember that others may be suffering and a small number of these people may turn to crime, bullying, or other negative behaviors to get there needs met.

The following story is an example of what I'm talking about, and this one goes from bad to good! One of my favorite newspaper columnists, A.C. Snow from the *Raleigh News & Observer,* shared this story with readers; it happened on a Christmas Eve many years ago.

James was 11 years old living with his mother, four siblings and an unemployed father. Times were hard for his family. It was Christmas Eve and he was selling newspapers on the corner hoping to collect a few dollars to buy gifts for his parents, brothers and sisters. It was getting late and the cold wind blew as he sold the last of his papers. Now his mind was on getting to the department store before it closed. Then a couple 'bullies' jumped out of the bushes, knocked him down, and stole his money.

As he sat on the corner crying, the newspaper's publisher, heading home for the night, saw him and asked what was wrong. James sobbed out his story. The publisher said, "James, come with me." They went straight to the department store. "Get something for your mom and dad," the man said. A few minutes later James had the two gifts but he still looked sad. "What's wrong James?" He replied, "I still don't have anything for my brothers and sisters." The kind gentleman said, "Well let's go to the toy department!"

As they left the store the good Samaritan asked, "Are you hungry?" They stopped by a café where James ate a couple hamburgers with all the trimmings, some fries, and a milkshake. Then, to top the evening off, James, for the first time ever, got to ride in a taxi that dropped him off in front of his house. He quietly placed his treasures under the small tree and went to bed.

James's evening went from bad (being bullied) to good (getting gifts for his family) thanks to the newspaper's publisher. Sure, James was happy and had gifts for his family. But do you know who received the greatest gift that evening? It was the kind man. One of the best feelings in the world comes from helping and giving to others.

The only person you can change is you. You cannot change others, but when you change, they often change.

ACTIVITY 53 PART 1: Bullying Behavior

Directions: This is a two-part activity that explores the actions of bullies. Gather in a small group and discuss.

Part 1: The List

Psychologist John Jensen notes that, bullying events occur along a continuum which children probably begin with:

1. emotionally isolated, distant, unconnected
2. Then move to being impolite, and then to:
3. inconsiderate
4. annoying
5. irritating
6. provoking
7. attacking
8. damaging
9. destructive
10. criminal

Jensen believes that most bullying acts fall into stages 4-6. Do you agree with him? Can you give some examples of annoying, irritating, and provoking behaviors of bullies? Have you ever dealt with bullies who went to stages 7, 8, 9, or 10? What are a few strategies that you've used to deal with bullies?

____

____

____

____

____

____

ACTIVITY 53 PART 2: Bullying Behavior

Directions: This is a two-part activity that explores the actions of bullies. Gather in a small group and discuss.

Part 2: Five Questions from Izzy

In his book *Bullies to Buddies*, Izzy Kalman asks the following questions. By yourself, answer the questions and then get with your group to compare answers. Izzy's answers are in the back of this book.

1. **The best person in the world to make bullies leave you alone is:**
   a) The President of the U.S.
   b) Your parents
   c) Your teacher
   d) The principal
   e) You

2. **When you get angry at bullies, the bullies are most likely to:**
   a) Feel bad about what they did and apologize
   b) Have fun and want to bother you again
   c) Get scared of you and leave you alone
   d) Cry

3. **Bullying happens to:**
   a) Kids in school
   b) Kids at home
   c) Adults
   d) People of all ages and relationships

4. **The first step to solving problems with other people is:**
   a) Blaming them for making you feel bad
   b) Blaming yourself
   c) Figuring out what you are doing wrong
   d) Complaining to adults.

5. **When people call you names and you don't try to stop them:**
   a) They will feel like losers
   b) They will feel like winners
   c) They will try to break your nose
   d) They will tell the teacher on you.

The Mystery of the Missing Fingers

Dr. Paul Brand wrote a book entitled, *The Gift of Pain*. You might be thinking, "How can pain be a gift?" Well, think about it. If you accidently put you hand on a hot stove and didn't feel any pain, you might keep your hand there for a while and suffer major burns. If you were walking barefoot and stepped on something sharp that cut your foot, if you didn't feel it, you might lose a lot of blood before noticing it. So, pain is your body's way of letting you know something is wrong. So be glad you can feel pain. Unfortunately there is a small group of people that can't feel pain in their hands and feet. These unlucky folks, known as lepers, have a disease called leprosy or Hansen's disease.

Leprosy is an infectious disease that has been known since biblical times. It is characterized by disfiguring skin sores, nerve damage, and progressive debilitation. Over the years lepers were treated poorly by others. Because people thought that they might get leprosy if they associated with them, the people would shun them. Lepers were forced to live in shacks, tents, and huts miles from town. The lepers had to wear bells to warn others that they were coming. Many were separated from their families. People refused to eat from bowls, dishes, and silverware used by lepers. Some people even believed that lepers were being punished by God for previous sins.

The worse suffering lepers had to cope with was the lack of use of their feet and hands. These body parts often lacked sensation. Nerve damage kept them from feeling pain. Dr. Brand traveled to India to do his best to help them. He performed numerous surgeries to straighten out their claw-like hands and deformed feet. Dr. Brand heard many stories how leprous fingers and toes simply "fell off." How could that be? The doctor was determined to solve this puzzle? Did fingers actually fall off?

Dr. Brand began his investigation. During his time in India he was aware that almost every leper was living in poverty. They lived in poor housing often infested with lice, bed bugs, insects, mice and rats. It seemed that the men and women with leprosy often noticed parts of their fingers missing in the morning. Dr. Brand had someone stay awake at night to find out what was causing the loss of fingers. The observer noticed that the lepers slept on dirt floors in their shacks. While they slept, rats would often come out at night a chew on the lepers' fingers. Because they had no feelings in their fingers they felt no pain and didn't realize that something was gnawing on them.

Once he solved the mystery he encouraged lepers to keep a cat in their sleeping room at night to keep the rats away. It worked. The lepers took his advice; no more fingers falling off at night! One of Dr. Brand's favorite patients was a young man named Raman. The doctor did several surgeries on Raman to straighten out his fingers. He was so happy with his limber hands and fingers that he wanted to travel to Madras to show his parents. Before he left for the trip Dr. Brand reminded him to take his cat along. A few days later Raman returned from his trip and entered the doctor's office. Both of his hands were covered in gauze bandages and soaked in blood. The sad young man said, "Doctor, I forgot to take my cat with me on the trip and a couple rats visited me in the night." Now Dr. Brand had to see if he could do anything to repair Raman's damaged hands. You can bet that Raman never went to sleep again without his cat nearby.

Dr. Brand could have opened an office back in the United States and gained much wealth but he chose to travel to an impoverished country to help a shunned group of people. His many surgeries, his compassion, and his discovery of the importance of cats made life better for hundreds of people.

ACTIVITY 54: Taking a Close Look at Our Fears, Worries and Concerns

Directions: In the story it was noted that many people had unwarranted fears of people with leprosy. What are a few of your fears? Remember, we all have a few. Following is a list of fears, worries, or concerns that many students have. How often do you worry about the following? Rate each one as follows:

0 = Never worry about this
1 = Rarely worry about this
2 = Sometimes worry about this
3 = Quite often worry about this
4 = Worry about this almost all the time

Note: You can do this survey privately or, if you wish, share your responses with others.

____ Getting good grades

____ My parents' health

____ Taking end of grade/course tests

____ Getting into college

____ Not being attractive

____ Getting a job after graduation from school/college

____ Water and air pollution

____ Global warming/ global change

____ Speaking in front of class

____ Friend, relative, family member dying

____ People talking/gossiping about me

____ Not having enough friends

____ Not having nice clothes

____ Being teased or bullied

____ Being in a car accident

____ Storms

____ Students stealing from me

____ Being alone

____ Heights

____ Snakes

____ Spiders

____ Being embarrassed/put down by a teacher

____ Being accused of cheating

____ Not living up to my parents expectations

____ Terrorism, war

____ Deep water

____ Flying in a plane

Other fears ________________________

____

"Yes, you must be polite!"

Cassie's father owned a small diner. While in high school she waited tables at the diner and started saving some of her wages for college tuition. Her father always told her to be polite to customers, no matter how rude they might be. Cassie learned that the nicer she was to customers, the larger the tips would be. Because of her pleasant personality and efficient service, many customers requested to have her as their waitress.

On weekends she worked the breakfast shift which meant she had to get up at 4:30am, drive to the diner, and prepare for the customers who started arriving at 6:00am. Every Saturday and Sunday morning an elderly gentleman by the name of Chuck Hansen would be waiting outside at 5:45am. None of the other waitresses wanted to wait on him. He was always grumpy, rude, complained about everything, and seldom left a tip. Cassie's dad made her be the unlucky one who had to serve him. She hated it. She pleaded with her father to let someone else be Mr. Hansen's server. Every day her father told her, "You will be his waitress and no matter how rude he is, you must be polite."

So when they opened the door at 6:00am, Mr. Hansen would be the first customer of the day and soon he started requesting Cassie. He would mumble, "I'm sitting in Cassie's section." Cassie would start getting sick to her stomach whenever she saw him walk in. She wanted to call him Mean Hansen instead of Chuck Hansen. For the next 30 minutes or so she had to put up with his rudeness and complaining. Many times she wanted to fuss at him but she remembered her father's order, "You must be polite." Mr. Hansen would say things like: "This coffee is cold! Hurry up; I'm going

to be late for work. This doesn't taste right! Take this back, it's too salty. Hustle up! I'm not coming back." But he always came back.

Every Saturday and Sunday for four years Cassie did her best to be polite to Mr. Hansen. She admitted that she hoped he wouldn't show up, but he always did. One morning to everyone's surprise, he wasn't waiting outside the diner at 5:45am. When the door opened at 6:00am, he didn't appear. Cassie sighed, smiled, and was glad he didn't come. She hoped he would never come back. Cassie's dad was puzzled. Where was he? "Were you rude to him, Cassie?" her father asked. "No, I was always polite, just like you told me to be." A few days later Cassie's father saw Mr. Hansen's obituary in the paper. He had died of a sudden heart attack. Cassie had mixed emotions. She was sad that he died but was glad that she would never have to wait on him again.

A few weeks later a tall man in a fancy suit, carrying a briefcase entered the diner. He spoke to her father who then pointed at her. The man walked up to her and introduced himself and asked, "Do you remember a customer named Chuck Hansen?" "Oh, yes!" she replied. The man went on to say, "Well, if you didn't know it he died a month ago and I'm the lawyer handling his will." Cassie told him that she was aware that he had died. The lawyer said, "Let me read to you a section of his will."

> ***I, Chuck Hansen, being of sound mind & body, wish to leave $50,000 and my car to Cassie Hays, a waitress at Del's Diner. She was always kind to me not matter how rude I was to her.***

Dad's advice paid off. Cassie was always polite to Mr. Hansen. Now she had a car and money for tuition. I agree with Cassie's father. Even though people may not be nice to us, we need to do our best to still be nice to them. It isn't easy and you may need 'tough skin.' But in the long run, kindness usually wins.

Even though others are rude to us, we should do our best not to return the rudeness.

ACTIVITY 55:
Venting frustrations

Directions: Almost every morning Cassie had to deal with Chuck's rudeness. I'm sure she did all she could to hold in her anger, but she must have had a few 'venting' strategies to help calm herself so she didn't lose her cool. How do you vent your anger? Following is a list of positive venting strategies. Put a check next to the ones that have helped you 'stay cool.' Next, pick your favorite one and explain why it works for you.

____ running/walking

____ yoga or meditation

____ biking

____ yell, scream, growl

____ holding breath for a few seconds/exhale

____ squeeze something

____ clinch fists

____ pray

____ play a sport

____ spend time with pet(s)

____ call or talk to someone

____ read

____ draw

____ write

____ other ____________________

My favorite venting strategy is ____________________

____

Because ____________________

____

____

____

____

Jack's Birds & Bible

It was Thanksgiving morning in 2007. It was Bob Murdock's first Thanksgiving morning without his mother. She had recently died after a long battle with cancer. This had always been his favorite holiday when he and his family got together and enjoyed his mother's tasty meals. Feeling down, he decided to pass up the traditional family gathering and go duck hunting. He wanted to alone; he missed his mother and often wondered how he could go on living without her in his life. He sat on the edge of a pond with his dog Sadie. After a while a few ducks started flying by. He shot one down and sent Sadie out to retrieve it. Sadie brought the duck to Bob. When he held it up he noticed it had an aluminum band around one of its legs. He read the words on the band: "Be Not Afraid: Only Believe-Mark 5:36-Jack Miner Foundation, Kingsville, ON."

Bob was immediately overwhelmed with emotion. He knew this was no coincidence. He felt that it was a message from his mother letting him know she was still with and that he need not worry about her. This event quickly lifted his spirit and he was able to enjoy the rest of the holiday. Now Bob became very interested in finding out more about Jack Miner, the bands, and the Bible scriptures.

Jack Miner was born in 1865 in Ohio and later moved to Ontario, Canada. He was one of eleven children born into a family that barely survived on their father's meager earnings from a brickyard. He never liked school because his was often teased about the way he talked, his red hair and freckles. He dropped out of school and worked with his father making bricks. In his free time he loved to get outdoors and enjoy nature. He was especially fascinated with ducks and Canada geese. He wondered how far they migrated every year and if the birds returned to the same place every year.

As he got older his interest in birding grew and he started to get more active in his local church. He loved birds and he loved his bible. He wondered, "How can I combine my two loves? How can I study geese and ducks and spread God's message?" At this time he had already started banding birds. He attached bands to the birds' legs as a way of monitoring their travels. He discovered that many birds returned to the same location every year. Some of his banded geese often traveled thousands of miles each year. He encouraged folks who found a banded bird to contact him. Eventually he discovered the way to combine his two passions. On each band he put a bible scripture. So whenever a hunter caught a goose or duck, he or she would get to read a scripture on the band. The scripture on the duck Bob Murdock caught had a great impact on him. Over the next few years Jack and the men at his bird sanctuary banded 50,000 wild ducks and 40,000 Canada geese, all with scriptures! Jack was convinced that many of the people who found his scriptures were positively affected.

People throughout the world began to recognize Jack and his accomplishments. In 1943 King George VI presented him with the "Order of the British Empire," which is the greatest achievement in conservation in the British Empire. Soon after he died in 1944, many U.S. newspapers rated him the 5th Best-Known Man on the continent behind only Henry Ford, Thomas Edison, Charles Lindbergh, and Eddie Rickenbacker. Jack proved that you can have more than one passion at a time and be successful in both.

Finally, here is one other interesting fact about Jack Miner. Even though he dropped out of school and could not read until the age of 35, there is a high school named after him in Scarborough, Ontario!

It is possible to pursue more than one passion at a time.

ACTIVITY 56:
Passions Can Lead To Careers*

Directions: By combining both his passions, Jack was able to pursue a successful career. Many of the following men and women were able to turn their passions into careers. Look at the names in the left column and see if you can locate the product for which they are famous. The answers are in the back of the book.

FAMOUS MEN & WOMEN

_____ 1. Orville Redenbacher
_____ 2. Henry Ford
_____ 3. Mary Kay Ash
_____ 4. Wally "Famous" Amos
_____ 5. Isaac Merrit Singer
_____ 6. James Folger
_____ 7. George Ferris
_____ 8. John Deere
_____ 9. Henry and Richard Block
_____ 10. Colonel Harland Sanders
_____ 11. William Keith Kellogg
_____ 12. Walt Disney
_____ 13. George Alfred Rawlings
_____ 14. William Hoover
_____ 15. Thomas Bromwell Welch
_____ 16. Herman W. Lay
_____ 17. Joseph Campbell
_____ 18. Milton Hershey
_____ 19. Ben Cohen & Jerry Greenfield
_____ 20. King C. Gillette

WELL-KNOWN FOR.....

a) breakfast cereal
b) tax preparation
c) cartoons
d) cosmetics
e) sewing machine
f) fried chicken
g) amusement ride
h) chocolate
i) vacuum cleaner
j) sporting goods
k) popcorn
l) fruit juices
m) farm equipment
n) coffee
0) soup
p) automobile
q) ice cream
r) chocolate chip cookies
s) razors, shavers
t) potato chips

**Adapted from Amazing Discussion Jump Starters, by Tom Carr (Youthlight Books, Inc.)*

500 Boxes of Shoes

The following story that I'm sharing with you is one of my favorites. It usually leaves the listeners astounded. They tend to be amazed at the surprising ending. It is based on a true story. I've heard several versions, but the best one came from a book about miracles and coincidences written by Yitta Halberstam.

Near the end of World War II the city of Prague (then the capital of Czechoslovakia) suffered several bombing raids. Over 1,000 people were killed and hundreds of buildings, factories, and historical landmarks were destroyed. Nazi Germany occupied most of the city. Gustave's home and the factory where he worked were among the buildings destroyed. Now he and thousands of others in the city had to find ways to survive. There were no jobs, factories, stores, and food was scarce. Gustave had a wife and four children. How could they survive with no income?

Gustave was desperate. He had to find a way to save his family. A traveler through the bombed out city told Gustave about a shoe store many miles away that was going out of business and the owner was trying to sell the few boxes of shoes left in stock. Gustave knew that many of the people in his neighborhood lacked good footwear. He thought that if he could secure enough money he could buy shoes and sell them for a profit; but he had almost no money. He borrowed money from several friends and relatives and he promised to pay them back. Then one morning his wife packed him food to last a few days. He hooked up his small horse to a wagon and set out for the long trip in the heat of summer.

It took Gustave three days to get to the shoe store. The owner told Gustave he had 500 boxes of shoes left. Gustave purchased them and turned around for the long trip back home. He was starting to feel optimistic. He could sell the shoes, pay back the people he borrowed from, and have money for his family. When he finally arrived home his loving wife greeted him with a smile and a hug. Gustave said, "Honey, look.

I have 500 boxes of shoes. We can sell them and feed the kids!" His wife opened a box. She looked puzzled. "Gustave, this box has two left shoes!" Gustave opened up a few more boxes, all with two left shoes! He cried, "Oh, no. We have 500 boxes of left-footed shoes. I must return to the store as soon as possible to get things straightened out. We can't sell these shoes."

Gustave suffered through three more days on the hot dusty trail. When he got to the store it was closed. Someone told him that the owner sold all his shoes and left town. Gustave broke down and cried. How was he going to explain this to his wife? He now had 500 boxes of worthless shoes and he owed friends and family money. He headed home for the long three day trip. He sobbed as he shared the news with his wife. She said, "Gustave you need to have faith. Don't give up. Go to the temple for ten days and pray. I've heard if you do that, something good will happen."

So he took her advice. He stayed in the temple for ten days. He cried a lot and prayed a lot. His wife brought him bread and water every morning and encouraged him to keep praying. At the end of the tenth day he was crying out loud. He did what she asked him to do and nothing good happened. Just about the time he was ready to leave, another man entered the temple. The man kneeled next to him and was also crying loudly. In fact, Gustave thought he was crying more than he was. He had to ask the man why he was so sad. The sobbing man replied, "A few days ago I traveled many miles to a small shoe store that was going out of business. I gave the man all my money for 500 boxes of shoes. When I got home I discovered I had 500 boxes of right-footed shoes. What am I going to do with them?" Gustave replied, "You've got 500 boxes of right-footed shoes from that store? I've got 500 boxes of left-footed shoes!" They left the temple to check the boxes. Somehow the shoes had gotten mixed up. All the pairs matched. They exchanged shoes. Now they both had 500 boxes of shoes, each with a left and right shoe!

Talk about a coincidence! Gustave's wife was right. She encouraged him to have faith and never give up. He sold all the shoes, paid back the people whom he owed, and had enough money to feed the family until the factories reopened.

ACTIVITY 57: Positive Self-Talk

Directions: What you say to yourself when the 'going gets tough' does make a difference. Positive self-talk and optimism can help you help you overcome setbacks. Following is a list of positive comments you can use in difficult situations. Check a few that you find useful. Then, if you have a favorite one of your own, share it with others.

_____ And this too shall pass.

_____ When I keep my cool, I'm under control.

_____ Tomorrow will be a better day.

_____ Maybe I'll learn something from my mistakes.

_____ I can't control others. I can only control myself.

_____ "The more time I spend on things I can't control, the less time I'll have to spend on things I can control." — John Wooden

_____ I refuse to blame others.

_____ Maybe it was my fault.

_____ I have learned to say "I'm sorry."

_____ I can forgive her/him.

_____ If at first I don't succeed, I try, try, and try again.

_____ I'm only human, and all humans mess up once in a while.

_____ I'll be able to look myself in the mirror in the morning knowing I did the best I could.

_____ All days are good but some are better than others.

My favorite positive self-talk is ______________________________

____

Risky Reading

People today don't realize how blessed they are when it comes to having access to reading material. Public libraries, school libraries, book stores, bookmobiles, and online books are just a few ways people can secure great reading material. Young people today are privileged to receive a free education and they are surrounded by teachers, parents, tutors, and volunteers who are anxious to help them become good readers. But that's not the way it was for slaves in our country who struggled to survive in the 1800's. In fact, severe punishments were inflicted on those who were caught trying to learn to read. For instance, in 1874 the state of Mississippi passed laws that allowed owners to cut off the hand or thumb of slaves caught reading or writing.

Despite possible punishments, slaves in our country wanted so badly to learn to read and write. Booker T. Washington's desire to learn was so intense that he compared a schoolhouse to paradise. He said, "I had no schooling whatever while I was a slave, though I remember on several occasions I went so far as the schoolhouse door with one of my young mistresses to carry her books. The picture of several dozen boys and girls in a schoolroom engaged in study made a deep impression upon me, and I had the feeling that to get into a schoolhouse and study in this way would be about the same as getting into paradise." How many children today compare school with paradise?

Many slaves took risks learning to read. G. W. Offley traded boxing and wrestling lessons with white men for writing instruction. Another enslaved boy, Richard Parker picked up old nails and traded them for marbles that he then used to pay white boys for reading lessons. Frederick Douglas, the well-known African American poet had a great strategy. He often traveled with a book and bread. When he met up with a white boy he would give him some bread in exchange for reading lessons. Some slaves had the job of taking their master's children to school every day in a carriage. These drivers picked up some reading skills just by listening to the children. Another woman recalled that her mistress and master spelled out information they did not want her to understand. Since she was unable to read, she memorized the letters and repeated them as soon as she could to her literate uncle. He then decoded her memories into words. Many enslaved people were able to get their hands on Noah Webster's Elementary Spelling Book. The book was so small that it could be hidden in their pockets or under their hats. One slave, Lorenzo Ezel told how he hid one of the small books under his hat while he was plowing the fields. Whenever he took a rest he would take out his book and learn a few words.

Most of the risk-taking took place on Sundays, especially when the master and his family went off to church. James Curry was a slave in North Carolina who was determined to learn to read. His master's son taught James a few basic skills but most of his learning happened on Sunday mornings. James would wait until he saw his master's wagon get out of sight, then he would head to bookshelf. He would carefully remove a book, being sure he knew exactly where to return it. He would turn the pages slowly, not wanting to tear anything or leave smudges. James knew that he would be beaten if the master knew he was reading the books. James would continue to read with one eye on the gravel road. As soon as he saw the wagon returning he carefully but the books back and snuck out the back door.

All the people mentioned in this story had such a passion for learning that they took great risks. What passions, desires, or goals do you have? Are you willing to take the necessary risks to accomplish them?

Successful people are those who climb out of their comfort zones and take risks.

ACTIVITY 58: Comfort Zones

Directions: Study the following scenario about a middle school girl by the name of Carole. Then answer the questions.

Several teachers have told Carole that she would make a good lawyer because she likes to gather facts and argue. Carole, an eighth grader, often dreams of being a famous lawyer but is afraid to take chances or risks to pursue that career. She likes living in her comfort zone. Every day after school she follows the same routine: homework, playing with her pets, dinner, television, computer time, reading in her room and then off to bed. She seldom leaves the house on weekends. Carole feels safe in the same day-to-day pattern. She'd like to be a lawyer but is afraid to climb out of her comfort zone.

List at least five risks that Carole might have to take if she wishes to become a lawyer.

1. ______________________

2. ______________________

3. ______________________

4. ______________________

5. ______________________

What is a career you would like to pursue after graduating? ______________________

Describe your personal comfort zone. ______________________

____

____

Can you climb out of your comfort zone? ❑ YES ❑ NO

List five risks you might need to take as you pursue your career goal.

1. ______________________

2. ______________________

3. ______________________

4. ______________________

5. ______________________

Looking for Snipers in Central Park

Many people are addicted to bird watching. They will get up at four in the morning, crawl through bushes, and wade through a swamp to catch a glimpse of a rare bird. True bird watchers are seen carrying binoculars, a bird identification book, and a notepad to chart their sightings. Lately, I have to admit, I've become a casual bird watcher, but there are some folks who are so hooked on this activity that they schedule family vacations around migration times. Others have called in sick to work or played hooky from college classes in order to sneak a few peeks at some pretty birds. The following story tells of a policeman who had a daily dilemma, go to work or go bird watching.

Howard and Sal were brothers living in New York City and they were avid bird watchers. They were also very competitive with each other. Each brother tried to top the other to see who had a longer list of sightings. They also competed to see which one was the first to sight certain species in Central Park. One year Howard became rather frustrated with his brother. It seems that Sal retired from his job while Howard continued working as a police officer. Howard thought this was unfair since Sal now had more time to search for birds.

Howard was teamed up with another policeman named Roger. They always worked the same shift and shared the same patrol car. Howard would always bring his birding binoculars and bird book to work. Many times Howard would sneak away from his duties to look for birds and there were days he showed up late. Roger always covered for him and never complained. Howard was so obsessed at bettering his brother that bird watching interfered with his job.

One spring day Howard heard rumors that a Magnolia Warbler was seen in a tree near a pond in Central Park. He had to spot that special bird before Sal, but there was one problem; on that same day the Emperor of Japan was scheduled to visit New York City. The Emperor's route had him going through Howard's patrol area of Central Park. All police officers were to be on duty to make sure the city's honored guest was safe. Howard knew he had to be on duty but, he had to find that warbler before Sal did!

The Emperor was scheduled to be in Howard's and Roger's district at two o'clock. As usual, Roger agreed to cover for Howard who rented a small boat to row out in the middle of the pond to search for the reclusive bird. At the last minute the mayor changed the Emperor's route and it entered Central Park an hour early. Roger was getting nervous as he noticed the police captain coming up the street to check on his officers. What could Roger say if the captain asked, "Where is Howard?" His boss stood next to him and glanced out over the pond and asked, "Roger, is that Howard in the boat looking up in the trees with a pair of binoculars?" Roger couldn't cover for his buddy this time and replied, "Yes, that's him." The captain mumbled, "Very interesting." Then he said, "Tell Howard I want to see him in my office first thing in the morning." Howard was finally caught shirking his duties. Roger knew his partner was in trouble.

Roger and Howard went to see the captain. Howard thought he might get fired. Instead, the captain shook his hand and said, "Howard, I want to congratulate you for your quick thinking yesterday. I never thought about positioning an officer in the pond to search the trees for snipers while the Emperor passed through the park. I'm proud of you. Please accept the $500 bonus and two paid days off from work." Roger couldn't believe what he just saw. He was the one who worked hard, never left his post, and always covered for Howard. And who got the bonus and time off?

Your mother is right, "Life's not always fair!"

ACTIVITY 59: Life's Not Always Fair!

Directions: Read the following scenarios. After each one note if you think the result was fair or unfair and why?

Danny practiced his baseball skills all winter long. He wanted so badly to make the middle school baseball team. He thought if he made the team his dad would be proud because his dad played Minor League baseball for the Atlanta Braves. The coach said he could have only 18 players. On the last day of tryouts one more player had to be cut. The coach had to decide between Danny and Myron; they had equal talents. Myron's father was the town mayor. The coach made his decision. Daniel was cut from the team.

❑ **Fair** ❑ **Unfair / Explain why.** ____________________

____

____

Florence was the single parent of five boys. Although she was a hard working lady, she never seemed to have enough money for food. Many times the boys went to bed hungry. One day she went to the local grocery store to buy food. She only had a little over twelve dollars. As the tired mother got in the checkout line with her seven items, she noticed a very well-dressed, rich looking man behind her. He had only one item and seemed to be in a hurry. She kindly said to him, "Sir, you can get ahead of me. " He never said thank you. When the cashier rang-up his one item, bells went off, confetti fell from the ceiling, and several employees shook his hand and the store manager said, "Congratulations Sir, you are our millionth customer. You've won $10,000."

❑ **Fair** ❑ **Unfair / Explain why.** ____________________

____

____

Business was slow at the restaurant. The manager had to lay off one of the waitresses. Hannah was always on time, never complained, hustled, had a nice smile and was good at writing receipts. Alexis was frequently late, seldom hustled, was moody, and made numerous adding errors. The manager said, "Alexis, I'm sorry but I'm not going to need you anymore. I hope you'll find another job."

❑ **Fair** ❑ **Unfair / Explain why.** ____________________

____

____

Chewing Gum: A Black Market Treasure

Balazs Szabo grew up in his beloved country of Hungry in the 1940's and 1950's. During most of those years Hungry was occupied by the Soviet Union. The invaders to his country were brutal and they forced their Communist rule onto everyone there. The oppressors controlled everything. Thousands of Hungarians died from starvation or were sent off to labor camps in Siberia. The Soviets took everything they wanted: food, clothing, farm animals, valuables, and they destroyed buildings. The Hungarian people were resilient and in 1956 they rebelled and prevailed even though 50,000 of their freedom fighters were killed or wounded. Balazs survived the rebellion and later moved to the United States.

During his childhood Balazs had to attend schools that were controlled by the Soviet Communist government. The Soviets tried to brainwash the children and tell them about the evils of America and capitalism. Balazs and his classmates were deprived of anything that came from the United States. Rarely did they have toys or candy. One day at lunch he noticed some of the students passing something around that was causing quite a stir. It was American chewing gum! The kids had to be very careful not to get caught with anything from America for fear of severe punishment. But Balazs wondered, "What is chewing gum?" He had never seen or heard of it before but it must be good as the kids passed the black market treasure around.

When it came to him he studied the shiny yellow package, pulled out the silver wrapping and its thin, light gray contents. It was his turn to smell it. What a rush of excitement to enjoy the smell of Wrigley's gum for the first time in his life. The students only had one piece to share so they struck a deal. Whoever took the gum home and chewed on it for one day had to pay a small fee, then, overnight, he had to soak the chewed gum in water, sugar, and toothpaste to renew its taste for the next chewer. When he took it home he had a hard time understanding why Americans would chew something without swallowing it and pay for it. He was afraid to chew it thinking he might accidently swallow it and get the other boys angry with him. Since he had no toothpaste to soak it in, he left it on his table overnight, though several times he did pick it up to smell the wrapper. He returned the gum the next day and he was relieved that he didn't get caught with it.

During the next few weeks the school was hit by an epidemic of influenza that was probably caused by the many students who shared the one piece of germ-infested gum. The school nearly shut down and the school officials had no idea what caused it. Only the kids knew. Balazs thought it was rather ironic that the kid who got access to the gum and who profited from it was one of the Communist Party members' children. Here was a child living with Communists' parents who was practicing capitalism. The boy was making money selling the use of his gum!

As Balazs shared this fascinating story with me it made me appreciate all the simple pleasures we have access to in this country. For most of us, we have no problem buying and enjoying a good piece of gum, but for young Balazs it was a rare treasure.

Be grateful for the little things in life.

ACTIVITY 60:
I'm grateful for...

Directions: In our story young Balazs was elated when he discovered chewing gum for the first time. These days it seems that everyone is chewing the flavorful treat. When I was a child I rarely had soft drink, maybe once a month if I was lucky. Now it isn't uncommon for some people to drink soda several times a day. For this activity interview someone who is at least fifty years older than you. Ask him or her to think of at least ten things that young people have today that they didn't have when they were your age. Then get with a few friends and brainstorm possible luxuries that children will have in fifty years that are unavailable to them presently.

Fifty years ago children didn't have...

1. ______________________
2. ______________________
3. ______________________
4. ______________________
5. ______________________
6. ______________________
7. ______________________
8. ______________________
9. ______________________
10. ______________________

In fifty years children my age will have...

1. ______________________
2. ______________________
3. ______________________
4. ______________________
5. ______________________
6. ______________________
7. ______________________
8. ______________________
9. ______________________
10. ______________________

The Messages

Story 1: An Alaskan Adventure

Message: Good things usually happen to good listeners. Bad things usually happen to bad listeners.

Source: A true story adapted from the book: *Into the Wild*, by Jon Krakauer (Villard Books, New York, 1996).

Story 2: The Persistant Pooch

Message: You will be surprised at all that you can accomplish if you are persistent.

Source: I came up with the idea for this story at a storytelling festival many years ago.

Story 3: Wilma and Glenn—They Did Not Run Out of Excuses

Message: Successful people seldom use excuses.

Source: The information on Glenn Cunningham comes from: *The Miracle of Motivation*, by George Shinn (Living Books, Illinois, 1994).

Story 4: The Slave and the Lion

Message: People and animals can develop strong, loyal, trusting relationships.

Source: The story is adapted from another version in the book, *When Elephants Weep*, by Jeffrey M. Masson (Dell Publishing, New York, 1995).

Story 5: The $0.59 Glider

Message: Don't be too quick to judge others and their actions.

Source: This event actually happened on the playground of a school I worked at a few years ago.

Story 6: A Tale of Determination

Message: When you are determined to reach a goal - you usually succeed in reaching it.

Source: This is a true story. I was inspired with the idea for this tale after watching a show about dogs on PBS.

Story 7: Shawn's Message... "Never Give Up!"

Message: Once you set a goal—don't quit or give up.

Source: This story is based on personally knowing this exceptional young man.

Story 8: Mind Games I

Message: Be your own person. Don't let your peers/friends "control" your mind.

Source: My idea for this story came from my observations and experiences with students.

The Messages

Story 9: Mind Games II

Message: Focus your mind and thoughts in a positive manner. Be optimistic.

Source: *Head First: The Biology of Hope*, by Norman Cousins (E.P. Dutton, New York, 1989) and *Mind, Body, Health* by Brent Hafer (Allyn & Bacon, Boston, 1996).

Story 10: The Snake and the Cowboy

Message: The solution to many problems is easier than we think.

Source: I first heard this tale at an all-night gas station in upstate New York. Definitely an old cowboy folk tale.

Story 11: A Great Nurse

Message: "You can get everything in life you want if you help enough other people get what they want." Zig Ziglar

Source: A picture in the newspaper of an elderly lady and a young girl gave me an idea that eventually became this story. The young girl was helping the woman across a crowded street.

Story 12: What's in your Pocket?

Message: Practice being creative.

Source: This true story was adapted from, *Some Pioneer Women Teachers of North Carolina*, by the Delta Kappa Gamma Society of North Carolina, 1955.

Story 13: Mistakes

Message: It's okay to make mistakes, as long as you learn from them.

Source: This is an example of a lesson I use with my students. I like to use names of famous people as it helps to motivate them.

Story 14: If Tomorrow Never Comes

Message: Tell those special people in your life that you love them every day.

Source: *"If Tomorrow Never Comes,"* a song by Garth Brooks, inspired me to write this story.

Story 15: Keep Honking

Message: Learning to work in a group and getting along with others are valuable skills.

Source: From personal observations of nature in action.

The Messages

Story 16: 499 In a Row

Message: You will be amazed at all the things you can accomplish if you only take the time to practice.

Source: I adapted this from an actual event described in: *Incredible Facts*, by Richard Manchester (Galahad Books, New York, 1985).

Story 17: The Genius and the Average Student

Message: To be "school-smart" is important, but you also need practical, common sense intelligence.

Source: This story is centered around an often told joke. I used a version of the joke from: *Successful Intelligence*, by Robert Sternberg (Simon & Shuster, New York, 1996).

Story 18: The Door of Opportunity

Message: Your Door of Opportunity is either closed or open - it's your choice.

Source: This true event is adapted from a story in: *One Minute Messages*, by Dan Clark (Sunrise Publishing, Salt Lake City, 1986).

Story 19: Animals As Teachers

Message: We can learn so much from animals.

Source: *A Cup of Chicken Soup for the Soul*, by Jack Canfield (Health Communications, Deerfield Beach, Florida, 1996). *The Man Who Listens to Horses*, by Monty Roberts (Random House, New York, 1996). *Peaceful Kingdom, Random Acts of Kindness by Animals*, by Stephanie Laland (Conari Press, Berkeley, California, 1997).

Story 20: Rolling Pin Smith's Sacrifice

Message: We often need to make sacrifices for our self or for others.

Source: A true story that came from the book, *Women & Men on the Overland Trail* by John Faragher, (Yale University Press, 1979).

Story 21: I thought It Was Your Dog!

Message: Don't be too quick to jump to conclusions. Make sure you know the whole story.

Source: I heard versions of this funny tale years ago. I changed it somewhat to stress my point mentioned in the above message.

Story 22: Monty's Essay

Message: Set goals and go for them. Don't listen to others who tell you that you can't reach your goals.

Source: This fascinating story comes from one of my all time favorite books: *The Man Who Listens to Horses*, by Monty Roberts (Random House, New York, 1996).

The Messages

Story 23: The Eagles vs. the Chickens

Message: Be careful in selecting your friends. They can influence you in a good way or a bad way.

Source: This comes from a rather common parable. I changed it to focus on peer relationships.

Story 24: Can Marshmallows Predict Your Future?

Message: Patience is a virtue. Slow down and control your impulses.

Source: *Emotional Intelligence*, by Daniel Goleman (Bantam Books, New York, 1995) and *Don't* by Jonah Leher (The New Yorker, May 18, 2009).

Story 25: Where's My Little Girl?

Message: Think before you act.

Source: Adapted from a story in: *One Minute Messages*, by Dan Clark (Sunrise Publishing, Salt Lake City, 1986).

Story 26: The 12-Year-Old-King

Message: To be trusted is one of the greatest honors in life.

Source: Adapted from a story in: *One Minute Messages*, by Dan Clark (Sunrise Publishing, Salt Lake City, 1986).

Story 27: The Million Dollar Bathroom Break

Message: Being embarrassed is part of life; it happens to everyone.

Source: A true event adapted from the book, *Small Miracles #2*, by Yitta Halberstam (Adams Media, 1998).

Story 28: "I Wish I..."

Message: You don't get what you wish for, you get what you work for.

Source: The idea for this story came after watching the New York City Marathon on television. I was amazed at the number of participants on crutches and in wheelchairs that completed the 26 mile run.

Story 29: The Missionaries and the Mambas

Message: Be careful when playing tricks or jokes on others. They can back-fire.

Source: I love this story. I first heard a version of it about 20 years ago at a party with friends. There are people in Africa who still believe this was a true story.

The Messages

Story 30: A Hug or a Handshake?

Message: Human touch is critical in the development of happy, successful, people, so hug a lot!

Source: *Mind, Body, Health*, by Brent Hafer (Allyn & Bacon, Boston, 1996). *Dare to Discipline*, by Dr. James Dobson (Tyndale House, Illinois, 1970).

Story 31: Should I or Shouldn't I?

Message: Sometimes in life you have to take risks.

Source: The idea for this story comes from my numerous travels to big cities. Millions of young people live in dangerous parts of these cities, and I'm sure many of them take risks every day just to survive. This story is based on a true event.

Story 32: Strength Coaching

Message: Everybody has a strength or something they are good at. Take advantage of it!

Source: Over the years, I've worked with many students who had strengths, but didn't use them. Teachers and parents need to "coach" these youngsters to help them build on their strengths. I wrote this story after reading about a famous barefooted runner from Ethiopia, who used his skill of running to become a hero in his country.

Story 33: Who is the Real Dummy?

Message: Be clever and creative when dealing with bullies and others who tease you.

Source: This story comes from two lessons I've used in the classroom numerous times.

Story 34: Mr. Lincoln's and Henry's Shocking Experience

Message: Don't tease others. We all have weaknesses.

Source: Adapted from: *The Top Ten List for Graduates*, by James W . Moore (Dimensions for Living, Nashville, 1997).

Story 35: The Worst Feeling in the World

Message: Nobody likes to be picked last.

Source: The poem *Choosing Sides* by Angelyn M. Hall. The poem was used with permission of the author.

Story 36: Compassionate Passengers on the Slave Ship

Message: Always practice the Golden Rule.

Source: A true story adapted from, *The Slave Ship* by Marcus Rediker (Penguin Books, New York, 2007).

The Messages

Story 37: A Cow Hit Our Boat!

Message: Always tell the truth!

Source: This story comes from an actual event reported on PBS.

Story 38: Rachel Never Told Her Dad

Message: Always give your best and avoid the "Loser's Limp."

Source: From my observation of hundreds of sporting events.

Story 39: You Should Have Listened to Your Mother

Message: Believe it or not, your parents/ guardians "nag" you because they love you.

Source: The idea for this story came from: *The Red Hourglass*, by Gordon Grice (Delacorte Press, New York, 1998). Many folks in Oklahoma will tell you this story is true.

Story 40: Javier's Rabbits

Message: You have to love yourself before you can love others.

Source: I wrote this story after reading about animal research in the book, *Love & Survival*, by Dean Ornish (HarperCollins, New York, 1998).

Story 41: Even Skunks Need Friends

Message: Be active in preserving our environment.

Source: I read about the skunk and yogurt problem in the newspaper. It's true!

Story 42: Cal Ripken Jr.'s Dilemma

Message: We all face dilemmas. Seek advice and support from those you respect.

Source: I heard about Cal's dilemma on a sports TV show.

Story 43: The $912,825 Mistake

Message: Don't overlook the little things in life.

Source: This true story was posted in jdnews.com, Jacksonville, NC, June 6, 2010.

Story 44: Help—The Pelican's Got My Dog!

Message: "No mind is thoroughly well organized that is deficient in a sense of humor."
— S.T. Coleridge

Source: A true happening heard on a cable television station program.

The Messages

Story 45: The Legendary "Goat"

Message: Everyday do something to improve yourself.

Source: I read about Earl Manigualt in the USA Today and I saw a movie about him on HBO.

Story 46: The Toothpaste Theory

Message: Words are the biggest motivators and de-motivators of people.

Source: I learned about the Toothpaste Theory in a lesson at church.

Story 47: I Promise to Pay You Back

Message: Keeping your promises builds trust and respect.

Source: This is adapted from an actual event I read about in a magazine many years ago.

Story 48: Women Can't Run a Marathon

Message: Everyone needs a hero.

Source: *Runners on Running*, by Rich Elliot (Human Kinetics, Champaign, IL, 2011).

Story 49: Today or Tomorrow

Message: Stop putting things off until tomorrow. Take action today!

Source: I thought of this story after reading a poem in the book: *Living, Loving, and Learning* by Leo Buscaglia (Ballantine Books, New York, 1982).

Story 50: El Nino and the Happy Cats

Message: When bad things happen, be patient. Often good things follow.

Source: I wrote this story after reading about the plight of cats in the August, 1998 issue of *Outside* magazine. It's true!

Story 51: A Roy Rogers Reputation

Message: A good reputation will get you further in life than gold and silver.

Source: Roy Rogers was a favorite of mine when I watched television as a kid. I decided to write a story about him after he died in the summer of 1998.

Story 52: Why Can't You be More Responsible?

Message: Responsibilities and privileges increase with age.

Source: This story is based on a true event adapted from the book, *Facing the Lion, Being the Lion*, by Mark Nepo (Conari Press, San Francisco, 2007).

The Messages

Story 53: From Bullies to Burgers

Message: The only person you can change is you. You cannot change others, but when you change, they often change.

Source: A true story by A.C. Snow in the *News & Observer*, Raleigh, NC, December 20, 2009.

Story 54: The Mystery of the Missing Fingers

Message: Everyone is afraid of something. We all have fears.

Source: A true story adapted from the book, *The Gift of Pain*, by Phillip Yancey and Paul Brand (Zondervan Publishing House, Grand Rapids, MI, 1993).

Story 55: Yes, You Must be Polite!

Message: Even though others are rude to us, we should do our best not to return the rudeness.

Source: I read about this true event in an Austin, Texas newspaper. I can't remember the date.

Story 56: Jack's Birds & Bible

Message: It is possible to pursue more than one passion at a time.

Source: A true story adapted from *Pro Hunter's Journal*, by Bob Murdock, January 30, 2010.

Story 57: 500 Boxes of Shoes

Message: Keep believing.

Source: I've heard several variations of this story. Many storytellers believe it is true.

Story 58: Risky Reading

Message: Successful people are those who climb out of their comfort zone and take risks.

Source: Most of the information in this story came from, *Self-taught*, by Heather Andrea Williams (University of North Carolina Press, Chapel Hill, NC, 2005).

Story 59: Looking for Snipers in Central Park

Message: Your mother is right; life isn't always fair.

Source: Based on a true story from the book, *The Falconer of Central Park*, by Donald Knowler (Bantam Books, New York, 1984).

Story 60: Chewing Gum: A Black Market Treasure

Message: Be grateful for the little things in life.

Source: A true event from the book, *Knock in the Night*, by Balazs Szabo (Lulu Publishing, 2008).

Activity Answers

Activity 3
1. c
2. I
3. a
4. h
5. e
6. b
7. j
8. I
9. N
10. G
11. M
12. K
13. O
14. D
15. F

Activity 6
1. X
2. O, H, X, I
3. A, G, H, J, L, T
4. Z, I, F
5. A, K, M, V, X
6. a) J
   b) I
   c) B
   d) T
   e) L
   f) Q
   g) P
   h) C
   i) U

Activity 10
One suggestion is to let some air out of the tires so the truck will be lower, then it can get through the underpass. You may come up with other ideas.
1. hog, dog
2. kitten
3. deer
4. duck
5. beaver
6. goat
7. hen
8. turtle
9. horse
10. snail, quail, whale
11. skunk
12. mink

Activity 33
1. 40 pennies, 2 dimes 8 nickels.
2. One thousand, nine hundred and ninety-one pennies are worth $19.91, which is almost $20.00.
3. Tommy's mother third child is named Tommy. What else could it be?
4. They are house/street numbers. Each digit costs 50 cents.

Activity 35
1. Dog
2. Gnu
3. Monkey
4. Beaver
5. Bear
6. Lion
7. Camel
8. Cat
9. sloth
10. horse
11. toad
12. mosquito

Activity 37
All 10 answers are true, according to the book, *The Best of the World's Worst*, by Stan Lee.

Activity 44
A. 3
B. 6
C. 10
D. 1
E. 7
F. 8
G. 9
H. 2
I. 4
J. 5

Activity 53
1. e
2. b
3. d
4. c
5. a

Activity 53
1. k
2. p
3. d
4. r
5. e
6. n
7. g
8. m
9. b
10. f
11. a
12. c
13. j
14. i
15. l
16. t
17. o
18. h
19. q
20. s